Genealogy Offline:

A beginner's guide to finding family history records that are not online

Claudia C. Breland

CONTENTS

Introduction

Imagine sitting at a wooden table in the state archives and opening up a bulging file folder, to find on top two long letters written by your great grandfather. Imagine receiving an envelope in the mail from a researcher at the National Archives and looking at affidavits on a Civil War pension file, for a soldier who was badly wounded at Gettysburg. Imagine reading in a land petition a description of land bought by a pioneer couple in Washington Territory who were later killed in an Indian attack.

The side-by-side explosions of interest in family history and the increasing numbers of original documents that can be found online can make the casual or serious family history researcher believe that "that's all there is". However, professional genealogists, who research daily in county courthouses, state and national archives, public libraries and historical societies, know that the majority of genealogy records are NOT online.

And what is online tends to lean towards names and dates. Which are all fine, but let's face it – aren't you fascinated with the stories of your ancestors? Don't you want to discover exactly when (and why) they left Ireland (or England, or France, or Germany) to come to America? Wouldn't you love to prove or disprove a family story? In family history, as in most other things worth doing well, stories matter. Details matter. And you will find those details in records that are not online.

Genealogy Offline:

In my 40 years of family history research, I have collected many documents and records that are not online. Some of them I've found in archives, libraries, museums, and historical societies. I've received digital images of records after emailing my question about an obituary or a will to a library or archive across the country. I've handled the original wills written by Revolutionary War veterans more than two hundred years ago. And I've received digital images from researchers examining microfilms at the Family History Library in Salt Lake City or original documents at the National Archives in Washington, D.C.

While this book is all about what, where and how – what these records are, where they are located, and how to obtain them – many times you will need to use online sources in order to pinpoint them. Whenever possible, I've included links to those resources, and encourage you to use them.

My area of expertise is genealogy and family history in the United States, so most of my examples will come from past research experience in this area. Many other countries have the same or similar archives, libraries, historical societies and museums, and my examples of US records can be used as signposts pointing the way – or giving you some ideas – to finding similar records abroad.

In each of these chapters, I will cover:

- What these records can tell you
- Where to find these records
- Online resources to help you find them
- Compelling examples

I hope you will be as excited as I am to discover new information about the people you're researching!

Claudia C. Breland

A Word about Sources

Many of the online sources you will find on your ancestors are not the original documents, but only indexes or transcriptions. It takes time and experience to realize when you are looking at a source that is an index, which is a good tool for pointing you to the original document, but is not the original document itself.

Indexes

For example, here is the index entry for Henry Hickox Chase, who died in Traverse City, Michigan in 1940:

Michigan, Death Certificates, 1921-1952," database, *FamilySearch* (http://www.familysearch.org: accessed 15 June 2013), Henry H. Chase.

Genealogy Offline:

While it does give a great deal of information, such as his name, date and place of death, and his parents' names, there is a lot that is not mentioned here. His cause of death, his address, the name of the cemetery, the name of the funeral home, and his date and place of birth are all important pieces of information for any complete family history.

When I ordered the death certificate from the Grand Traverse County Clerk, this is what I received:

Grand Traverse County, Michigan, death certificate 95 (1940), Henry H. Chase; Grand Traverse County Clerk, Traverse City.

The death certificate tells me that his mother was born in Ohio and his father in New York, his cause of death, the name of the cemetery in Bear Lake (which is in Manistee County, not Grand Traverse), his exact age, and the fact that he died in the Traverse City State Hospital.

Transcriptions

In the same fashion, learn to recognize when you are reading something that is a transcription (or an exact, word-for-word copy) of an original document. Family history books are full of transcribed wills, deeds and other records. For example, the Last Will and Testament of Deliverance Slason, in *Michigan Genealogical Notes*, gives no citation as to its source. Did the author have the original will when he transcribed it? Did he find it at the county courthouse, or was it at the state archives? Did he copy from another source, which would make it a copy of a copy?

Deliverance Slason will, *Michigan Genealogical Notes*, (n.p.:1933), p.133; digital image; *Heritage Quest* (accessed from public library, 3 September 2013).

This is a typed copy of the will, which was most likely handwritten. Any time something is copied, the possibility of errors is present.

Family Trees

Since the internet became a useful tool for researching your family history, online family trees have been popping up all over the place. You can find them on Ancestry, and websites such as Tribal Pages, My Heritage, FamilySearch, and many others.

If you're lucky, these family trees will cite their sources. More often than not, they don't, and you're left guessing where the tree owner got those names and dates! Use the family trees you find as clues, to point you toward possible original sources, but don't take them as gospel truth.

Many of the resources you can find online are actually indexes, abstracts (that is, summaries) or transcriptions. Whenever you find a piece of information online, stop and ask yourself, "Is this the original document?" If not, make the decision to go after it!

Social Security Applications

When Franklin D. Roosevelt signed the Social Security Act in 1935, it was not only an assurance of income for Americans as they aged; it was also the beginning of a great set of records. If your parent or grandparent died after 1962 after having worked for several years, chances are they may have filled out a Social Security application. Thanks to the Freedom of Information Act, you can obtain a copy of any application, as long as the individual is deceased.

What They Are
At first glance, these records would seem to be just another source of names and dates. However, they differ in several important ways from the usual sources of birth, marriage and death dates. Social Security applications are one of the least-known and least-used records, and they are not online!

Valuable Information
One of the most important aspects of the Social Security application (or SS-5, as the form is called) is that the applicant, for the most part, filled it out themselves, with the knowledge they had about themselves and their parents. This included their full name at birth, their current name, current place of residence, date and place of birth, and their parents' full names, including (if known) the maiden name of their mother.

Another important clue that may be overlooked is the date they signed the application, and their current address and employer at that time. So if there's a hole in your timeline for your ancestor in the 1930s and 1940s, this application just might be a crucial piece of information.

This Social Security application was the key to discovering someone's ancestry. Nelson is a very common name, especially in Minnesota. Here Earl Nelson gives his date and place of birth, enabling me to find him on the 1900 census with his parents, who were of Swedish descent.

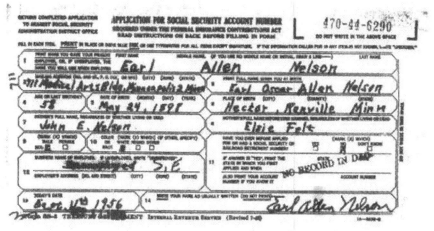

Earl Allen Nelson, SS no. 470-44-6290, 11 September 1956, Application for Account Number (Form SS-5), Social Security Administration, Baltimore, Maryland.

Occasionally the Social Security Administration will send a printout that is a reverse image, like this one. Sophia (Dzido) Jagush was applying for a Social Security number decades after the death of her husband, when she was in her 80's. Although this form states she was born in New Jersey, she was actually born in Austria; on various census records her birthplace is recorded as Austria, Galicia, and Poland. The variability of information in records is another good reason to retrieve all the records you can find!

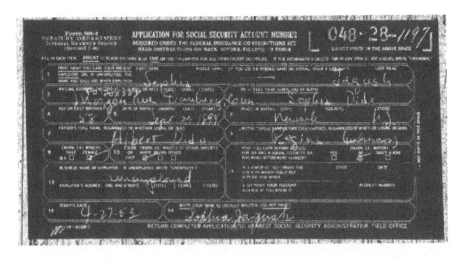

Sophia Jagush, SS no. 048-28-1197, 27 September 1953, Application for Account Number (Form SS-5), Social Security Administration, Baltimore, Maryland.

When Social Security registration became mandatory, many corporations typed up the form from the information they had in their files, and called in the employee to sign it. A typed application such as this one calls for more careful examination of the information on it, as it may be secondary information.

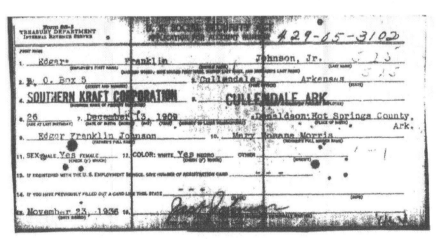

Edgar Franklin Johnson, Jr., SS no. 429-05-3102, 23 November 1936, Application for Account Number (Form SS-5), Social Security Administration, Baltimore, Maryland.

Claudia C. Breland

Not everyone who had the information filled it in. When he was 15 years old and just starting a new job, Gene Leroy Arntzen had to fill out a Social Security application. He knew his father's name, but probably didn't know his mother's maiden name, so he just put "(unk)" (unknown). He probably could have asked his mom or another family member, but didn't.

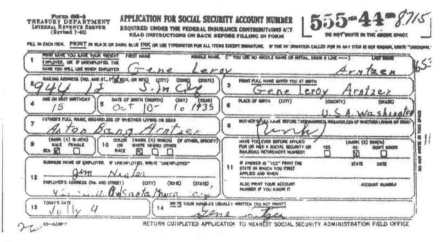

Gene Leroy Arntzen, SS no. 555-44-8715, 4 July 1951, Application for Account Number (Form SS-5), Social Security Administration, Baltimore, Maryland.

This is a good time for me to emphasize something that I have discovered in my years of research, and that has been stated several times by Dr. Thomas W. Jones, editor of the National Genealogical Society Quarterly in his lectures and presentations:

There is no such thing as a completely accurate record!

Keep in mind that people lie and people forget. Often you don't know who the informant is on a record, or if that informant knew himself, the accuracy of the information he was giving. Approach every record with an open and questioning mind!

Where to Find a Social Security application

These Social Security applications are not online, and probably never will be. In order to request a copy of the record, which is known as the SS-5, it's necessary to know the name of the person (for women, both maiden name and name at the time of death) and if possible, their Social Security number.

At this time, the cost is $27 if you have your ancestor's Social Security number and $29 if you don't know it. You can find your ancestor's Social Security number on several online databases:

Ancestry (subscription): http://www.ancestry.com
Steve Morse: http://stevemorse.org/ssdi/ssdi.html
FamilySearch: http://www.familysearch.org

Here is Earl Nelson's Social Security Death Index entry on FamilySearch:

Social Security Administration, "U.S. Social Security Death Index," database, *FamilySearch.org*
(http://www.familysearch.org: accessed 24 June 2013), entry for Earl Nelson, 1977, SS no. 470-44-6290.

In the past couple of years, the Social Security Administration, in response to public fears about identity theft, has changed the rules about what information they will release. They have started redacting (or blacking out) the names of the parents of the individual, unless the person in question was born more than 120 years ago. So, if your grandfather was born in 1940 and died in 2000, his parents could theoretically still be alive.

How to Order an SS-5

By far the easiest way to order this record is online, directly from the Social Security Administration, using a credit card. You can do this by searching online for "SSA-711", which is the Request for Deceased Individual's Social Security Record. You can find this form and other FOIA (Freedom of Information Act request forms here:
http://www.ssa.gov/foia/request.html.

Genealogy Offline:

Make sure that you have all the information about your person of interest, including their Social Security number.

If there is any possibility that the Social Security Administration would black out the parents' names, then your best option is to fill out the form and mail it in with your payment. Be sure to include whatever proof you have that the parents are deceased. You can find the form here:
http://www.socialsecurity.gov/online/ssa-711.pdf.
Proof that the parents are deceased could be a census record or obituary, or any other record that shows they were born more than 120 years ago.

The Social Security application is an important piece of evidence for any of your ancestors who died after about 1960 after having worked for several years. Even if you think you know the information that would be on it, it's worth retrieving!

Claudia C. Breland

Land and Property Records

Consider these words:

"But Sir I would implore your Aid and assistance, as far as you can to a Man that has left Europe, and brought Seven Sons and two Daughters to this Country one of My Sons was Shot Dead by A young Indian In August 1820 And This is my oldest son's Land that is in Contemplation And He is Dead. I have five living yet…"

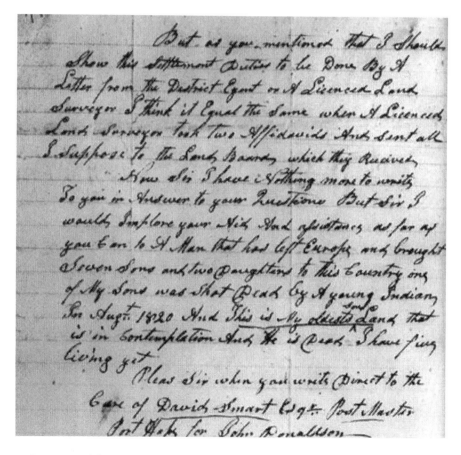

John Donaldson Land Petition, 1844, Volume: 166, Bundle D3, Petition 79, Microfilm C-1881, Ref: RG 1 L3, Archives of Ontario, Toronto, Ontario, Canada.

They were written by John Donaldson, an emigrant from Ireland to New York, and then from New York to Monaghan, Ontario. In this message to the General Council, he was asking them to let him buy the land belonging to his son James Donaldson, who had died two years before this was written in November of 1844.

Where did I get it? Not online, but from a researcher who found it on microfilm at the Archives of Ontario. This is just one example of the fascinating information that can be found in land records.

What They Are

Land records are an extremely important tool for genealogical research, and entire books have been written about the subject. What follows is a general, brief overview.

There are two basic types of land records: land obtained by an individual from the federal or state government by purchase or by a grant, and land acquired by a private sale. Beginning in colonial days, grants, homesteads and cash entry sales were all ways that settlers could acquire land. One way that Revolutionary War soldiers and veterans of later wars were compensated for their service was the award of land in the developing states, which were called bounty land warrants. Military Bounty Land Warrants are an important set of land records that prove an individual's service and often give details of his family after the war. The Homestead Act of 1862 gave land to pioneers – such as the family of author Laura Ingalls Wilder – for agreeing to farm and improve the land for a set period of time.

One of the overriding reasons our ancestors came to this country was for the freedom to own their own land. Even if it was only a parcel of 40 acres in the woods of Minnesota, a man and his growing family could call it their own. By buying, improving, and then selling land, immigrants could improve their standard of living and become upwardly mobile – something that was not possible in the countries they came from.

Valuable Information

Land records are especially important when other records (such as vital records or census records) are absent, contain incorrect information, or are incomplete. If a courthouse burned, the birth and death records may not have been recreated, but the land records probably were.

Very often, land was transferred within a family – a father would deed several acres "in consideration for the love, good will and affection I bear my son." The executors of an estate would sell the land jointly and have the sale recorded by the county clerk. Often the occupations of the buyer and seller (also known as the grantee and grantor) would be noted, along with their place of residence.

Land records have the potential for answering questions and solving puzzles. Often relationships were spelled out or indirectly assumed, as in this deed from Clearfield County, Pennsylvania. Isaac Thompson Sr. and "Keziah his wife" are selling land to Isaac Thompson Jr. This land record was on a microfilm of deeds from Clearfield County.

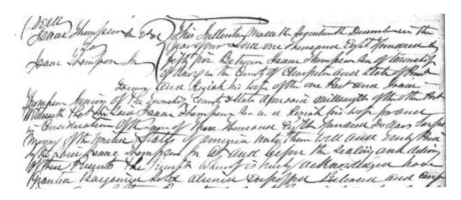

Clearfield County, Pennsylvania, Deed Book P:515, Isaac Thompson Sr. to Isaac Thompson Jr., 17 Dec 1854, FHL microfilm 1436418.

Where to find land records

Land records are kept in many different repositories; here are some examples of where you can find them.

National Archives, Washington, D.C.

Records of the original sale of land in federal (or **public**) land states by the government are held at the federal level – usually at the National Archives in Washington, D.C. or one of its branches. There are indexes online, but for the most part the documents themselves are not. The General Land Office website that I mentioned before: (http://www.glorecords.blm.gov) is an index to **some** of the land records sold by the Federal Government. The states included in the BLM index are:

Alabama
Alaska
Arizona
Arkansas
California
Colorado
Florida
Idaho

Illinois
Indiana
Iowa
Kansas
Louisiana
Michigan
Minnesota
Mississippi
Missouri
Montana
Nebraska
Nevada
New Mexico
North Dakota
Oklahoma
Ohio
Oregon
South Dakota
Utah
Washington
Wisconsin
Wyoming

Although the final document awarding Riley E. Breland his 160 acres in Mississippi is online at the GLO website, housed at the National Archives in Washington D.C. are 28 pages of documents, contained in this packet:

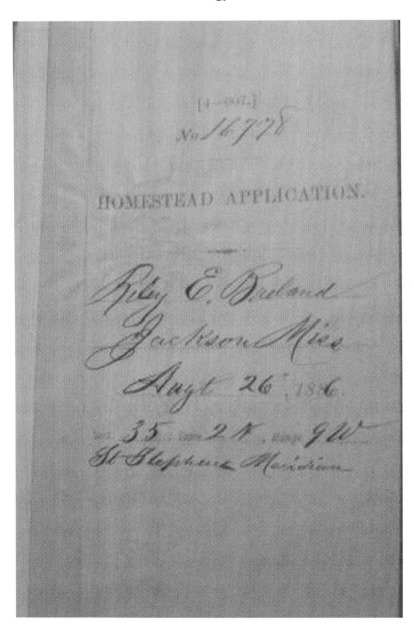

The file includes his application, with his signature:

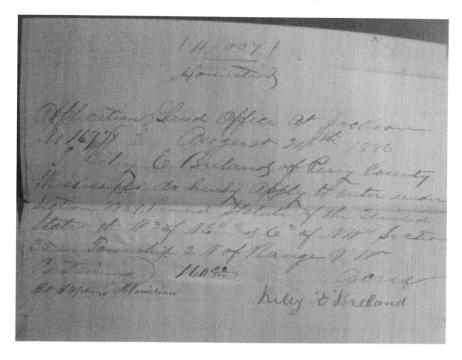

Riley E. Breland (Perry County), homestead file, application no. 16,778, Jackson, Mississippi, Land Office; Land Entry Papers, 1800-1908; Records of the Bureau of Land Management, Record Group 49; National Archives, Washington, D.C.

As with most applications of this kind, there are depositions from friends who could testify that Riley had improved the land, building a house, kitchen, smoke house, 3 corn cribs and stables, and that he had not been absent from the land more than a day or two in the five years he'd lived there.

When it was time for Riley to make his final application and get the land awarded to him, a notice was put in the local newspaper.

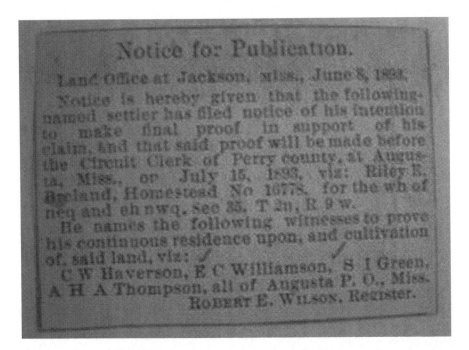

Notice for Publication.

Land Office at Jackson, Miss., June 8, 1893.

Notice is hereby given that the following-named settler has filed notice of his intention to make final proof in support of his claim, and that said proof will be made before the Circuit Clerk of Perry county, at Augusta, Miss., on July 15, 1893, viz: Riley B. Breland, Homestead No 16778, for the w½ of ne¼ and e½ nw¼. sec 35, T 2n, R 9 w.

He names the following witnesses to prove his continuous residence upon, and cultivation of said land, viz:

C W Haverson, E C Williamson, S I Green, A H A Thompson, all of Augusta P. O., Miss.

ROBERT E. WILSON, Register.

Often these original land grant records include several pages. There may be affidavits from friends of the applicant, who knew him and could vouch for his character. There may be a description of the improvements made to the land, such as a list of the buildings and crops. And if the person applying was literate, there will be a signature.

Military Bounty Land

Military Bounty Land Warrants are housed at the National Archives in Washington, D.C. Revolutionary War veterans, veterans of later wars, their widows and sometimes their heirs were awarded land in the growing country as a form of payment.

John Wasson was a private who served in Virginia during the War of 1812, and died in 1823, just before his pension was approved. His widow Ellen applied for his pension, and in 1855 she requested the bounty land warrant that was due him. This document was in the Revolutionary War pension records that are online at Fold3:

State of Virginia
County of Rockbridge
     On this 3rd day of April A.D. 1855 before me a Notary Public within and for the county and State aforesaid, personally appeared Ellen Wasson, aged about 80 years, a resident of Rockbridge, State of Va. who, being duly sworn according to law, declares that she is the widow of John Wasson, deceased, who was a private in the revolutionary War being the identical person named in a original certificate of pension now in her possession. No. 1673, "Recorded in the Pension office on the Roll of Pensioners under act February 3d, 1853, Page 113 Vol. A" and to which she refers as proof of her said husbands service, marriage and death. She declares that she is still a widow. She makes this declaration for the purpose of obtaining the bounty land to which she may be entitled under the "Act approved March 3d 1855"
     Ellen (x her mark) Wasson

John Wasson (Pvt., Col. Campbell's VA Regiment), pension no. W.1007, Revolutionary War Pension and Bounty-Land Warrant Application Files; Department of Veterans Affairs, Record Group 15; National Archives, Washington, D.C.; digital image; *Fold3* (http://www.fold3.com: accessed 4 August 2013).

The actual bounty land warrant is an elegant document, and not available online. This is stamped with the number of acres being awarded, and has the name of the soldier and/or the name of the heir receiving it.

Ellen Wasson, widow of John Wasson, (Pvt., Col. Campbell's VA Regiment, Revolutionary War), bounty land warrant no. 27661 (Act of 1855, 160 acres); Military Bounty Land Warrants and Related Papers; Records of the Bureau of Land Management, Record Group 49; National Archives, Washington, D.C.

National Archives regional branches

In addition to the National Archives in Washington, D.C., there are several branches located throughout the country. You can see these locations and the areas they cover here: http://www.archives.gov/locations/.

The Seattle branch of the National Archives holds federal land records for Washington, Oregon and Idaho. These date back well before Washington became a state in 1889, to the early 1840's when it was still part of the Oregon Territory. There are Master Plat maps for each township, and the corresponding land patents are available on microfilm. The Seattle Genealogical Society created a volume of abstracts (short summaries) for each land patent, which was indexed by surname.

One of the land patents on file there is one brought by the heirs at law of Elizabeth Brannon, who with her husband William Brannon had settled on Sections 6 & 7 of Township 21 North, Range 5 East. If you're familiar with the online General Land Office website (http://www.glorecords.blm.gov), you will see the index entry here:

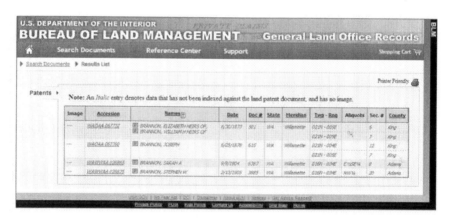

Bureau of Land Management, "Land Patent Search," digital images, *General Land Office Records* (http://www.glorecords.blm.gov/PatentSearch: accessed 20 July 2013), Elizabeth Brannon (King County, Washington Territory), Accession WAOAA 067732.

However, the full record of this patent is recorded on M815, roll 99, page 616 to 630: over 15 pages of documents telling the story of this couple. The original land patent was filed by William H. Brannon in April 1855. He gives his birth date and place (1832 in Ohio) and the date and place of his marriage to Elizabeth Brannon: 29 December 1853 in King County, Washington Territory. The next pages were depositions by Elizabeth's father, Michael Livingston, who attested to the fact that William and Elizabeth and their infant daughter were killed by Indians on their land in 1855. Along with information about the Brannons, Michael Livingston testifies to the effect that his wife, Elizabeth's mother, died in Benton County, Oregon in 1856.

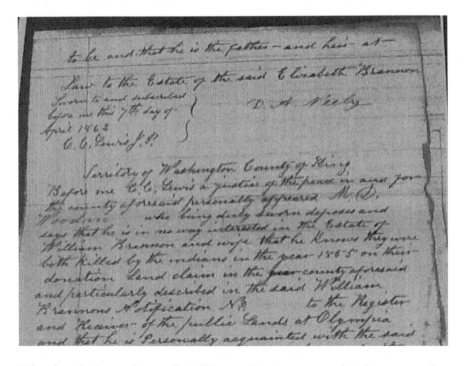

File for heirs-at-law of William H. Brannon, land patent for Washington Territory, Sections 6 and 7 of Township 21 North, Range 5 East. M815, roll 99, page 616. National Archives and Records Administration, Seattle.

Also at this branch of the National Archives are plat maps, which give a visual image of the land being described in the document:

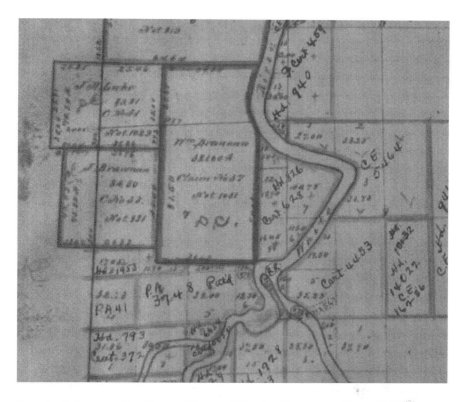

Land plat map for Township 21 North, Range 5 East, Willamette Meridian in Washington Territory. Record Group 49, Vol. 28, Box 31, National Archives and Records Administration, Seattle.

You can take this plat map a step further, and by using a website such as Earthpoint:

(http://earthpoint.us/TownshipsSearchByDescriptio n.aspx), you can plot the land on Google Earth. By doing that, it's evident that the land the William and Elizabeth Brannon farmed is now part of downtown Auburn, Washington.

Family History Library, Salt Lake City

There are thousands of microfilmed land records at the Family History Library in Salt Lake City. You can either order the microfilms online, using their library catalog to look them up, or hire a researcher who works there, who can send digital images by email. (See Using the Family History Library Catalog.)

In New Ipswich, New Hampshire, the heirs of Abijah Foster sold their interest in the land they inherited to Peter Fletcher.

"Know all Men by these presents that we William Hodgkins yeoman & Elizabeth his wife, Tabitha Foster widow of Ephraim Foster yeoman, Joel Russel, Yeoman & Mary his wife & Hepzibah Foster, Spinster, all of New Ipswich, in the county of Hillsborough & State of New Hampshire, In Compensation of Three Thousand Pounds [....] to us in hand paid by Peter Fletcher of New Ipswich aforesaid Gentleman..."

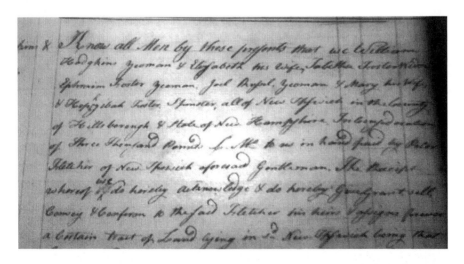

Hillsborough County, New Hampshire, Deed Book 8:7-8, 30 Apr 1779, Ephraim Foster et.al. to Peter Fletcher, FHL microfilm 0,015,934.

Land records can serve to confirm a family story. My great-great grandfather Marshall Jackson Chase was allegedly badly injured in a logging accident in Michigan in the 1860's, and could not work for years after that. When I looked at microfilmed land records for Clinton County, Michigan, I discovered that it was not Marshall Chase, but his wife Mary Ann who sold their land in 1865, in order to move her husband and family to Lansing.

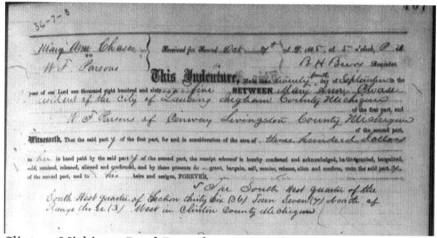

Clinton, Michigan, Deed Records, v.31:407 (1865), Mary A. Chase to W.F. Parsons; FHL microfilm 987,127

And this particular land record has Mary Ann Chase's signature; proof that she could read and write. Comparing signatures on several documents is a good way to determine if the same man signed them, or if it was two different men. Many such records were signed by an "x" if the person signing was illiterate or too sick to write his name.

Land records can indicate a person's previous home. In 1778, Daniel Foster, "late of Andover, Essex County, Massachusetts Bay" sold land in Hillsborough County, New Hampshire:

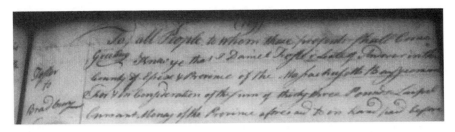

Hillsborough, New Hampshire Deed Book 6:189, 4 April 1778, Daniel Foster to Barnabas Bradbury, FHL microfilm 0015933.

State Archives and Libraries

In the years before the Revolutionary War, the thirteen colonies granted land to the colonists, in order to extend their boundaries. These states are:

Connecticut
Delaware
Georgia
Maryland
Massachusetts
New Hampshire
New Jersey
New York
North Carolina
Pennsylvania
Rhode Island
South Carolina
Virginia

In the years following the war, other states joined these colonies in granting land to their settlers:

Maine
Vermont
Kentucky
Tennessee
West Virginia
Texas
Hawaii.

These twenty states are considered "**State Land States**"; these records will be held at the state level.

State archives should always be checked for land records. The Oregon State Archives in Salem has land records for Clackamas County; land records for other Oregon counties are held at the individual county courthouse. The Washington State Library has the Washington State land entry files on microfilm. It may take some investigative work in the state you're researching to find where the land records are kept.

The Puget Sound Regional Archives has records of private land sales in Pierce County. When Levander Curtis died in 1921, his children sold the family home in Tacoma. These records are indexed in the big, heavy index books that were used back in the 1920's.

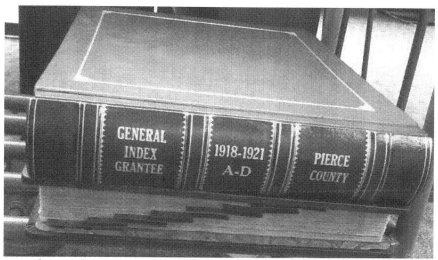

On the index page, under Curtis is listed the transaction, which gives the volume and page numbers of the actual deed.

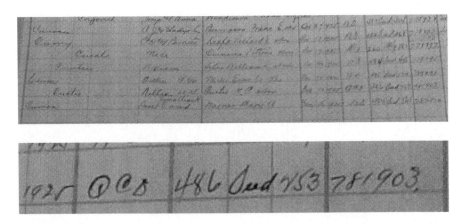

Pierce County, Washington Grantor Index A-D, 1918-1921; entry for Nellie Curtis et. al.; Puget Sound Regional Archives, Bellevue, Washington.

When the deed is found in Volume 486, page 253, it fills the bottom half of the page. It tells me that this is a quit-claim deed, in which H.P. Curtis (the executor of his father Levander Curtis's estate) and his wife Leila received ten dollars from Nellie Curtis and Jessie Stenberg (his sisters) in order to give up his claim to the house in Tacoma. If I didn't know that Nellie and Jessie were his sisters, this would give me additional names to research for a possible family connection.

Pierce County, Washington Deed Book 486:253, Nellie Curtis and Emil Stenberg to H.P. Curtis (1925); Puget Sound Regional Archives, Bellevue, Washington.

County Courthouses

A piece of land may be sold or granted once by the federal government, and those records will be at the National Archives or one of its branches. However, the vast majority of land transactions were private ones, between individuals. Those records will generally be found at the county courthouse.

Kitsap County, Washington was formed in 1857 from parts of King and Jefferson counties – and none of the land records are on microfilm at the Family History Library. At the county level, historic land records are on reels of microfilm at the Kitsap County Auditor's office. For some older records it's necessary to ask for the book to be brought out from the back room.

For example, in 1878, Michael Thielan was one of the parties in a warranty deed; here is the entry in the grantor/grantee index for 1874-1889.

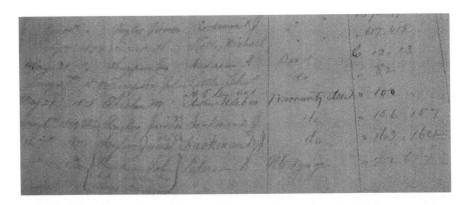

The actual deed is on microfilm at the Kitsap County Auditor's office:

Kitsap County, Property Records C:100, Michael Thielan warranty deed (1878), Kitsap County Auditor's Office, Port Orchard.

My grandfather Maurice L. Reed was a truant officer in Lansing from the 1920's until 1952. Every summer he took his family camping on the shores of Crystal Lake, in northwestern Michigan, paying $1 per week for the prime lakeshore property and the hill behind it, studded with wild berry bushes, columbines, and morel mushrooms. In July 1940 he bought the land from the owner's widow, Winifred Snell, for "One Dollar and other valuable considerations". When I wanted evidence of the purchase of the land, I called the Benzie County Courthouse, and they mailed me a copy for $10.

Benzie County, Michigan, Deed Book 70:278, Winifred Snell to Maurice and Ruby Reed; County Clerk's Office, Beulah.

How to Obtain Land Records

Just in the last few years technology has made it possible to order federal records online from the National Archives, which you can do here:

Genealogy Offline:

http://www.archives.gov/research/order/

However, ordering from the National Archives can be very expensive. Currently it costs $50 to order a land entry file, and $80 for the first 100 pages of a Civil War pension record. Whenever I want a copy of a record from the National Archives, I ask one of several researchers who are there on a weekly basis to obtain it for me. The cost is much less, I get it faster, and instead of getting black and white photocopies I get digital color images, sent to me by email or Dropbox.

To obtain copies of records from a branch of the National Archives, you can go to their published list of researchers here:

http://www.archives.gov/research/hire-help/

You can also send an email to the archives branch directly, asking if they have the record you want; often this saves time.

You can also contact one of the members of the National Capital Area Chapter of the Association of Professional Genealogists, here:

http://www.ncac-apg.org/

For land record located at a county courthouse or archives, you can email them directly to ask about getting copies. They may refer you to local researchers.

The volunteer website US GenWeb (http://www.usgenweb.org) is a good place to check for addresses and phone numbers of county courthouses.

As well as being a source of information (direct or indirect) about our ancestors, land records give us a glimpse into the lives they led in past years. If land was important to them, the records they left behind should be just as important to us.

Wills and Probate Records

The Last Will and Testament of Zerah French, which is on file at the Puget Sound Regional Archives in Bellevue, Washington, is a little different from other wills written during the same time period. In it he dispenses with the traditional opening used through the years, "In the name of God, Amen", and begins instead with "I, Zerah French, of Green [River and County of] King and Territory of Washington..." In this will he makes provisions for two sons and a daughter, and asks that "it is furthermore my wish that I be buried beside my Dear Old Wife on the Old Homestead on Green River. Then he says, "under no consideration shall there be any Christian Religious ceremonies over my remains."

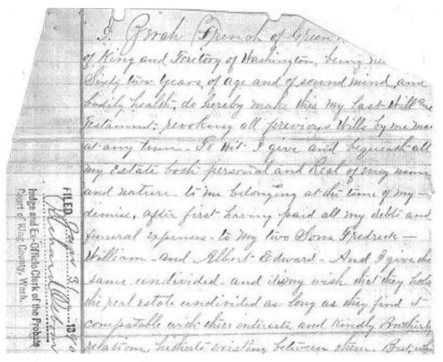

King County, Washington Territory, probate case files, no. 979, Zerah French (1889), will of Zerah French, 31 January 1889; Puget Sound Regional Archives, Bellevue, Washington.

What They Are

Whether or not your ancestor made a will, if he or she died leaving property of any kind, there is usually a probate file. This can consist of several different documents, including a will (if there is one), the court's appointment of an executor or administrator, an inventory of the estate, appointment of guardians for minor children, newspaper notices to creditors, and receipts for expenses paid by the executor. You may also find a letter from the executor appointed by the testator (writer of the will) giving up their responsibility for handling the estate, or a letter from a potential heir stating their claim.

These probate files are generally kept in the courthouse of the county where the decedent made the will – which is not necessarily where he or she died. For example, the will of Zerah French (1827-1890) was submitted for probate in King County, Washington, where he lived and owned property. However, the will itself was written in San Bernardino, California, and Zerah died in Michigan while on a trip back East to visit family members.

Valuable Information

Probate records can contain a wealth of information. If the deceased (the testator) left a will, he may have named his wife, children, and grandchildren. He may have named a son-in-law to be the executor of his estate, or named another relative to be a guardian for his minor children.

Wills can provide fascinating details of what daily life was like at that time. In Joseph Donaldson's 1872 will, he made sure to provide for his widow, directing his son thus:

2nd I give devise and bequeath unto my second son James George Donaldson all and singular that piece or parcel of land and premises being comprised of the Fourth lot in the fifth concession of the township of South Monaghan aforesaid Charging and requiring him to pay the following: To his

Mother during her natural life or as she remains my Widow yearly and every year to pay unto her the sum of Fifty dollars of good and lawfule money of Canada together with the following produce, viz: Twelve pounds of tea, Fifty pounds of Sugar, Five hundred pounds of good flower, Ten bushels potatoes, Thirty pounds Beef or Mutton, One Barrel pork, Twelve pounds of Carded Wool and milch and butter sufficient for her own use allso all fire wood she shall need.

I also desire that my wife possess during her natural life the east half of the house I now live in together with all furniture thereon and her bed, bedding, Bureau & looking glass and the east half of the garden. I allso desire and require my son James George to provide my wife with a conveyance at all times that she shall desire the same to and from church and at least four times each year to and from Port Hope or Peterborough...

Joseph Donaldson, Last Will and Testament, *United Counties of Northumberland and Durham Surrogate Court Records*, Microfilm no. GS 1, Reel 1106, File no. 1272, Archives of Ontario, Toronto.

The last will and testament of James Oliver, Revolutionary War veteran in Rockingham County, North Carolina, is a good example of the details of the family that you might find in a will. In it he names his wife and then each of his children:

> *"To John Oliver and his heirs forever, Also to
> the Heirs of Polly Goff who intermarried with
> William Goff, to them forever. Also I give to the
> Heirs of Susanna Oliver who intermarried with
> James Lumbrick to them forever, also I give to the
> Heirs of Sally Shepherd who intermarried with
> Wm Shepherd to them forever. I also give to
> Samuel Oliver and his heirs forever, and also to
> Elizabeth Oliver and her heirs forever..."*

Here it is important to note that a **copy** of this will is now online at FamilySearch – the copy that was written in the will book kept by the county clerk, at the time the will was submitted for probate. The **original** document that James Oliver dictated in 1840 and then signed with his mark is located in the North Carolina State Archives at Raleigh, NC. Any time you read a will that is in a book with other wills, at the county clerk's office, you can be fairly sure that it's a copy.

Where to Find Probate Files

Probate records may be at the original county courthouse, or moved to the state archives, or may have been microfilmed.

The last will and testament of wealthy attorney Emil Steinberg is on microfilm at the Pierce County Courthouse in Tacoma. First I had to look up the case number in a huge, heavy bound book that was the index to probate records:

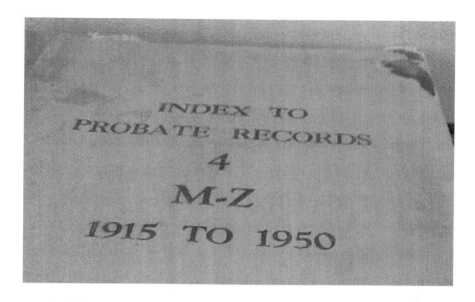

His entry in the index looked like this:

Pierce County, Washington, Probate Index M-Z, 1910-1950, Emil Stenberg.

I wrote down the case number (36248) and presented it to the clerk, who retrieved the 16mm microfilm for me. The film was reversed, white on black:

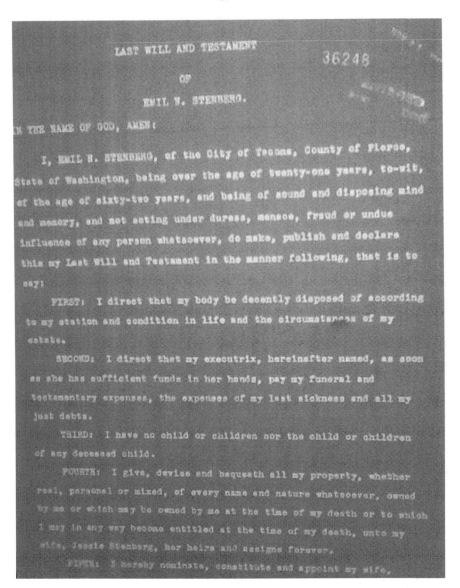

LAST WILL AND TESTAMENT

36248

OF

EMIL N. STENBERG.

IN THE NAME OF GOD, AMEN:

I, EMIL N. STENBERG, of the City of Tacoma, County of Pierce, State of Washington, being over the age of twenty-one years, to-wit, of the age of sixty-two years, and being of sound and disposing mind and memory, and not acting under duress, menace, fraud or undue influence of any person whatsoever, do make, publish and declare this my Last Will and Testament in the manner following, that is to say:

FIRST: I direct that my body be decently disposed of according to my station and condition in life and the circumstances of my estate.

SECOND: I direct that my executrix, hereinafter named, as soon as she has sufficient funds in her hands, pay my funeral and testamentary expenses, the expenses of my last sickness and all my just debts.

THIRD: I have no child or children nor the child or children of any deceased child.

FOURTH: I give, devise and bequeath all my property, whether real, personal or mixed, of every name and nature whatsoever, owned by me or which may be owned by me at the time of my death or to which I may in any way become entitled at the time of my death, unto my wife, Jessie Stenberg, her heirs and assigns forever.

FIFTH: I hereby nominate, constitute and appoint my wife,

Pierce County, Washington, Probate file 36248, Emil Stenberg, 1941, roll no. 568, Tacoma, Washington.

The cost of copies at courthouses and archives can vary considerably; at the Pierce County Courthouse copies are 50 cents per page, and at the Puget Sound Regional Archives they are 25 cents per page. I have had good results taking pictures of the screen with my iPad or digital camera. Policies on copying or photographing records vary from place to place, so be sure to ask permission!

The will of Arthur Denny, one of the founders of Seattle, is kept in a file at the Puget Sound Regional Archives, a branch of the Washington State Archives:

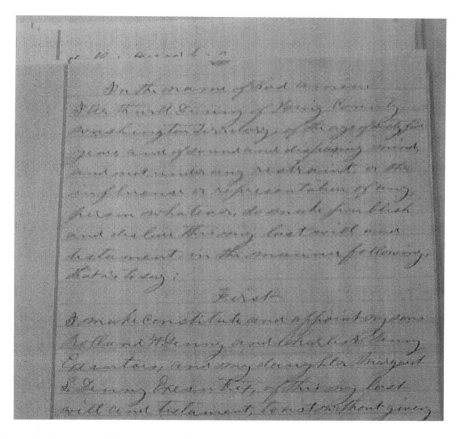

King County, Washington, Probate File 3111, Arthur Denny (1899); Puget Sound Regional Archives, Bellevue, Washington.

The staff at the archives prefer that patrons view the probate records on the microfilm, which is not nearly as readable:

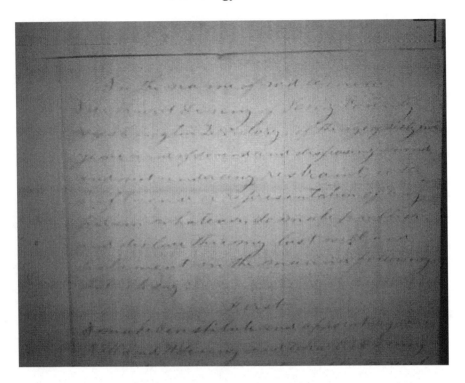

King County, Washington, Probate File 3111, Arthur Denny (1899), roll PA-136, Puget Sound Regional Archives, Bellevue, Washington.

Because the Washington State Archives has a central location and five regional branches, which branch a will is housed at depends on the county where the will was entered into probate. When I emailed the main Archives in Olympia, asking about the will for Dora Phillips, who died in Olympia in 1925, they emailed it to me in a PDF, at no charge:

IN THE SUPERIOR COURT OF THE STATE OF WASHINGTON

IN AND FOR THE COUNTY OF THURSTON

FILED

In Superior Court Thurston Co. Wash

APR 30 1926

DEPY. CLER

IN THE MATTER OF THE ESTATE)

OF) No. 3333

DORA A. PHILLIPS,) ORDER SETTLING FINAL ACCOUNT
) AND DECREE OF DISTRIBUTION

Deceased.)

. . . .

This cause coming regularly for hearing in open Court this
30th day of April, 1926, on the petition of Edith Christopher,
praying for distribution of said estate, and on the hearing of
the final account of said Edith Christopher.

And it appearing to the Court from the testimony introduced
that said final report is in all things true and correct and
should be approved and confirmed.

NOW THEREFORE IT IS HEREBY ORDERED, That the said report
be and the same is in all things settled, approved and confirmed.

And it appearing further to the Court that Dora A. Phillips
died at Olympia, Thurston County, Washington, on the 23rd day
of July, 1925, leaving surviving her a daughter, to-wit: Edith
Christopher and two grand-children, to-wit: Reve Phillips and
Irene Phillips, said Reve Phillips and Irene Phillips being the
children of a deceased son of the said Dora A. Phillips, deceased,
and that she left no other child or children nor the child or
children of any deceased child, and that all of said children are
over the age of twenty-one years and competent mentally.

That the said deceased left a Will wherein the said Reve
Phillips and Irene Phillips were each given the sum of One Dollar
($1.00), and all the rest, residue and remainder of said property
was devised and bequeathed to her only daughter, Edith Christopher,
which Will was duly admitted to probate in said cause and the
said Edith Christopher was appointed as executrix pursuant to
said Will and qualified as such.

Thurston County, Washington, Dora Phillips Probate File 3333,
1926, Washington State Archives, Olympia, Washington.

Many wills and probate files have been microfilmed and are located at the Family History Library in Salt Lake City. This is where a researcher located the estate records for Jacob Painter of Chester County, Pennsylvania. This is a petition for administration of his estate, since he died intestate (without a will):

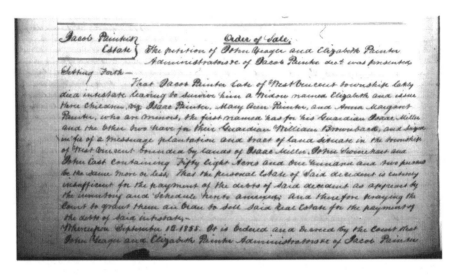

Chester County, Pennsylvania Records of the Orphans Court, 24:136, Jacob Painter (1855), FHL microfilm 550724.

Wills and probate records are extremely important pieces in any complete family history. While more of them are coming online at various websites, there are many more of them that are not. These records are worth looking for, for the treasures they contain!

Vital Records

I still remember the first vital record I ever requested. My mother's mother, Bessie Randall Stoelt, died in December 1931 when my mother was only 5 months old. My grandfather remarried the following year, and so there were a lot of things my mother didn't know – most importantly, her mother's cause of death.

So shortly after I became interested in family history, I requested Bessie's death certificate from the state of Michigan:

Michigan Department of Health, death certificate 14001 (1931), Bessie Blanch Stoelt, Division of Vital Statistics, Lansing.

This certificate provided my mother with some very important primary information, including her mother's cause of death and the cemetery where she was buried. And today, more than 80 years after Bessie Stoelt's death, this death certificate is still not online.

What They Are

Vital records are the records of the most important events in a person's life: birth, marriage, and death. There is no national system of keeping track of these records. Each state began a centralized system of recording at different times. Massachusetts has some vital records going back to the late 1690's. Michigan began recording statewide in 1867, and in Mississippi it wasn't till 1915 (or after) that vital events were reported. Often, even before the state required reports, vital events were recorded at the county or township level.

Valuable Information

Vital records can vary considerably in the information they contain. The earliest records were handwritten, sometimes on loose sheets of paper and sometimes in a book that was kept at the county clerk's office. Many records, especially from before the nineteenth century, contain only the basics: for a marriage, the name of the bride and groom, the name of the minister, and the date. Even when a record is supposed to have further information (such as parents' names and places of birth, for a death record), the presence and/or quality of that information depends completely on the informant.

Always look for vital records for the siblings and children of your ancestors! If the informant for your great-grandfather's death certificate did not know his parents' names, perhaps the informant for his younger sister did. What's more, perhaps that younger sister was the one to write down and preserve the family stories.

Look for the record that happened the nearest to the date you're looking for. My grandmother Ruby Chase Reed's marriage record and death record both indicate her birth date was Feb. 25, 1892, but her birth record revealed that she was actually born in 1891.

Where to Find Vital Records

The first place to head for a vital record that is not online is the county where the event took place; some states (such as Connecticut or New York) have these records at the town level. When I requested the 1830 marriage record for Newcomb Randall and Louisa Clark from the Lorain County, Ohio, clerk, they sent me a photocopy of the entry in their book, and a statement of authenticity.

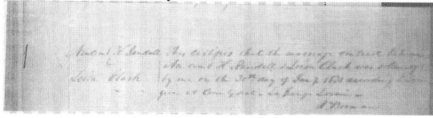

Lorain County, Ohio, Marriage Records, 1:62, Newcomb Randall and Louisa Clark (1830), Court of Common Pleas, Elyria, Ohio.

And although Ohio County Marriages are online at FamilySearch, this one is not listed.

Sometimes the county clerk will send you a typed copy of the record they have, filling in a standardized form. Realize that this is a copy, and not the original. Also, this may be an extract of some of the information on file, and not the entire record.

New Jersey, Registrar of Vital Statistics, Death certificate 89-24, John A. Thompson (1930), Morris County Clerk, Chatham, New Jersey.

In this case the certificate is unusual because the space for "Social Security Number" has "Unknown," because John Thompson died in 1930, before Social Security was invented! Any time you have a copy of a record, the possibility for errors exist.

Some vital records might be housed at the state archives. When I requested a copy of my great-grandfather's 1913 marriage record from the Washington State Archives, they scanned and emailed it to me:

Genealogy Offline:

Thurston County, Washington, Marriage Return #3646 (1913), James L. Reed and Dora Phillips; Washington State Archives, Olympia, Washington

Marriage records come in many different forms – you may find an application for a marriage license, a marriage certificate, and/or a marriage return, which is the officiant's return of the record to the state, verifying that the marriage took pace. Any or all of these can have different information. The parents of the bride and groom are more likely to be listed on the marriage license; the names of the witnesses may be listed on the marriage certificate or register.

In addition to state archives, some counties in the United States have county archives. Housed at the King County Archives in Seattle, in an archival folder, is their treasured "little black book" that contains the earliest marriage records in Seattle when it was still part of Oregon Territory. This fragile book contains 37 records dating from 1853 through 1869. The first marriage recorded was that of David Denny and Louisa Boren, which took place in the Denny home on 23 January 1853.

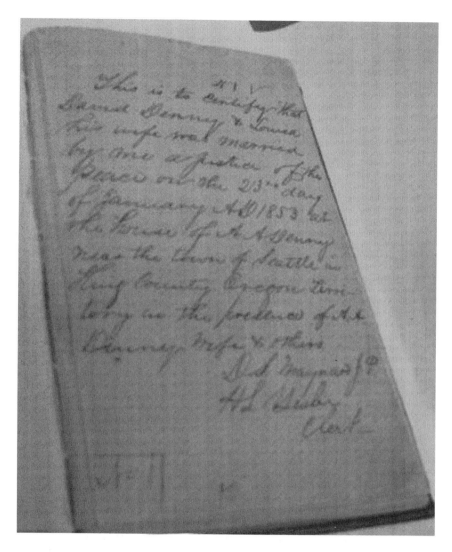

David Denny and Louisa, marriage registration, 23 January 1853, Book 1, record 1, King County Archives, Seattle, WA.

With today's easy access to thousands of records that are online, it is easy to overlook the fact that many records are available only by writing and requesting a paper copy. Depending on the time and location of the record, the information provided can vary. But even if you think you know what might be on a vital record, it is important to obtain these records for every person you're researching.

Online Finding Tools for Ordering Vital Records

Here are two of my favorite finding aids for writing to a state agency for a vital record:

Centers for Disease Control "Where to Write for Vital Records"
http://www.cdc.gov/nchs/w2w.htm
This database gives information on birth, marriage, divorce and death records for each state:
> When statewide recording began
> Address
> Phone number
> Cost of copies
> Website
> Where to write for earlier records

Online Searchable Death Indexes & Records: A Genealogy Guide
http://www.deathindexes.com
This is a complete listing, by state and then by county, of all the online resources for death records, obituaries, probate records and cemetery records that are online. At the bottom of the listing for most states is a link to the state website with instructions on ordering vital records online or by mail.

It's usually faster and less expensive to order a vital record at the local level, rather than from the state health department. For example, ordering certain vital records from the California Department of Public Health can result in a wait time of over 6 months; a request to the Los Angeles County Clerk will be filled in about two weeks.

When I found a gravestone inscription for a previously unknown child of Eliza and Augustus Randall, Emerson Randall, who died in Pentwater, Michigan, at the age of 18 days in 1877, I sent for his death certificate from the Oceana County Clerk, which cost $10. Ordering it from the Michigan Dept. of Health in Lansing would have cost $26.

Be aware that several states, in an effort to crack down on identity thieves, are making it much harder to obtain copies of vital records. The state of Iowa, for example, requires a copy of your driver's license and a notarized statement that you are the person named on the document or a close relation.

A cousin of mine, at my request, sent for his grandfather's 1971 death certificate from the state of Colorado. It took him two tries, because the state required copies of his driver's license, his birth certificate, and his father's death certificate, in order to prove that he was related.

Family History Library

The Family History Library has microfilmed records from courthouses all across the country and that includes the birth, marriage and death registers kept by county clerks. Before you order microfilm of a birth or death register, be sure to check online at FamilySearch to see if they have been digitized. See "Using the Family History Library Catalog."

Vital records are among the first records that genealogists use in their pursuit of knowledge about their ancestors. Remember to obtain the records for collateral family members, as those may answer questions or fill in the blanks.

Court Records

If you've been in your county courthouse lately, you know what a variety of business gets transacted there. In my local courthouse (one of two county courthouses in King County, Washington) we can pay property taxes, get a license for a business, get a license for a pet, file a lawsuit against a company or a person, start eviction proceedings, attend a criminal trial, finalize an adoption, and get a divorce. All of these actions result in records and paperwork, which are saved for future reference. Today these records are generally saved electronically, but our ancestors created court records that are like windows into the lives they lived.

Since 1725, when the first courthouse was constructed in King William County, Virginia, courthouses have been an important center of legal activities at the county, state and federal level. There are courthouses in every county of the United States; sometimes more than one.

Jurisdiction Matters

Where these records are kept depends a great deal on where the case was tried, and the subject of the case. A county courthouse may be the location for the District Court and the Superior Court; the federal courthouse is where cases are tried that involve the US Government or one of its agencies.

What They Are

Civil cases can include lawsuits, paternity cases, personal injury, medical malpractice, disputes over land or property, adoptions, divorces and guardianships. Criminal cases are brought against the defendant by the state or the country, depending on the crime that was committed.

Records of the proceedings in a court case, whether civil or criminal, will include the initial complaint brought by the plaintiff, a copy of the summons issued to the defendant (and proof that the notice of the summons was delivered or published), the record of the court proceedings, and the decision of the judge or jury. All of these papers will have the date and case number.

Some court records will be at the federal level, not the state level. If the case involves kidnapping across state lines, robbing a post office, bankruptcy, or anything else that involves a federal law, the records will be kept at the National Archives or one of its branches.

Valuable Information

If you're looking for good stories about your ancestors, court records are full of them! In any kind of court records, details of your ancestors' lives will be revealed. Witnesses in a trial or civil suit may include family members, important dates and events may be recorded

Where to Find Court Records

The first place to look for court records, naturally, is at the county courthouse. At the Pierce County Courthouse in Tacoma are rows of books containing indexes to civil records:

Most (if not all) of their court records are on microfilm; you have to use the heavy index books to look up the case numbers in order to request them.

Many county courthouses are microfilming and/or placing digital images on their own in-house computers, in order to protect fragile documents. At the Lewis County courthouse in Chehalis, Washington, after I requested a file, I was shown to a computer in the research room where the digital image (209 pages of a criminal complaint) was displayed:

In the Superior Court of the State of Washington

WARRANT

Superior Court, State of Washington v. Claud H. Ryan, case no. 1321 (1927), digital image; Lewis County clerk, Chehalis, Washington.

State Archives

Often, older court records have been moved to the state archives. The Oregon State Archives in Salem has large ledger books full of records for Power of Attorney. In 1899 Peter Rabor of Sitka, Alaska Territory, assigned his power of attorney to Oscar Forsburg, of Oregon City in Clackamas County.

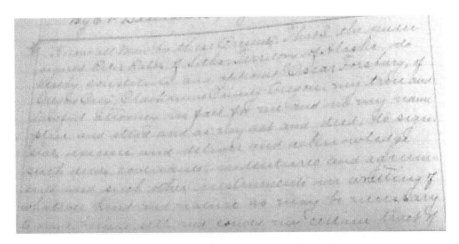

Clackamas County, Clerk of Circuit Court, Power of Attorney, 1:110-111 (1899) Peter Rabor to Oscar Forsburg, Oregon State Archives, Salem, Oregon.

Also at the Oregon State Archives are land, military, probate, naturalization and vital records.

At the Puget Sound Regional Archives in Bellevue, Washington the original records detailing Sarah McDonough's 1899 committal to Western Washington Hospital for the Insane are available to view:

King County Washington Superior Court, file 3112, Sarah McDonough (1899), Puget Sound Regional Archives, Bellevue, Washington.

National Archives

Any court records resulting from a case in federal court will be found at the National Archives in Washington D.C. or one of its branches. These kinds of cases can cover things from mail fraud, theft from a U.S. agency, a lawsuit against the United States, kidnapping across state lines, forgery, and others.

Just to give you an idea of how much material is stored at one branch of the Archives, here is a glimpse of just a fraction of their holdings:

The National Archives branch in Seattle, Washington has rows of shelves of federal records, and over 70,000 rolls of microfilm, some of which are not yet digitized or online. It is the record retention center for Washington, Oregon, Idaho, Montana and Alaska.

In November of 1890 in the Ninth Circuit court, District of Montana, George Ross took the Montana Union Railway Company to court, alleging patent infringement on his invention, called "An Improvement to Dump Cars". The summons to the railway company read in part, "The said action is brought to recover from you said defendant the sum of $18750.00 actual damages, alleged to have been sustained by plaintiff by reason of the infringement by you of certain Letters Patent...". George Ross won his lawsuit, and the court awarded him $7,500 plus court costs of $174.86. The packet at the National Archives in Seattle includes both the original handwritten documents and a typed transcription.

Ninth Circuit Court, District of Montana, case no. 10, George Ross vs. Montana Union Railway Company (1890), National Archives, Seattle, Washington.

Bankruptcies are always filed in federal court, and generally include a list of the creditors the plaintiff is seeking relief from.

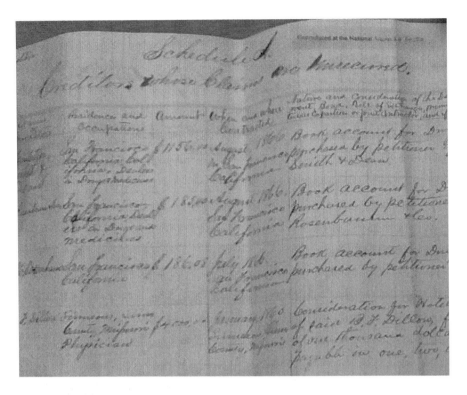

U.S. District Court, Portland, Oregon, case no. 46, Jas. W. Murray (1878) Schedule of Creditors, Petition for Bankruptcy, National Archives, Seattle, Washington.

Some of these bankruptcy cases can be quite large, resulting in a stack of paperwork that has been preserved:

There are many laws in the U.S. Code that can be (and have been) broken, causing people to be brought to trial. In 1878 Clara Newsom was accused in the Oregon District Court of making counterfeit gold two dollar coins. In 1896 Julius Hurel was subpoenaed to the Montana District Court and accused of selling a quart of alcohol to an Indian. In 1875 John Madlock was brought before the court on charges of cutting timber on federal land for his own use.

And in 1897 C.A. Wasson was accused of "depositing in the United States Mail for transportation and delivery a certain letter containing obscene, indecent, vulgar and filthy matter, in violation of Section 3.895 of the Revised Statutes of the United States." In this particular file are depositions from various mail carriers who handled the letter, including one, who when the letter was handed to him, stated, "I remember this letter. I soiled this letter by carrying it in my pocket with a piece of buttered toast."

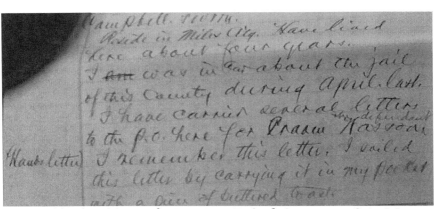

District Court of Montana, United States vs. C.A. Wasson (1897), National Archives, Seattle, Washington.

Court records of every kind and at every level can be great sources of information about your ancestors – how they lived, how they treated their neighbors, and how they kept (or broke) the law. Court records are worth exploring for the information they contain!

Military Records

I've received many Civil War pension records in the years I've been doing research, but none of them affected me more than the pension file of Andres Franklin of Cattaraugus County, New York, who fought with the 64th regiment of the New York Infantry. Among the papers was a deposition from a fellow soldier, Rodney Crowley, who testified:

On this twentieth day of May A.D. 1864 before me a justice of the Peace in and for said county duly authorized to administer oaths personally came Rodney R. Crowley who being by me duly sworn, deposes and says that he resides in the town of Randolph County aforesaid & is 27 years of age; that he is the identical Rodney R. Crowley who was lately Captain of Company "B" in the 64th Regt. NY Vols. in the service of the United States; that on the second day of July A.D. 1863 he was captain as aforesaid and in command of his said company in the Battle of Gettysburg in the State of Pennsylvania; that he is well acquainted with Andres Franklin applicant for Invalid Pension and that said Franklin was a private in said Company "B", 64th Regt. NY Vols.: that on the said 2nd day of July 1863 the said Franklin was doing duty in the ranks of his said company and was seriously wounded in the left leg by a minie rifle ball while charging upon the enemy with his said company and regt. under a heavy infantry fire, at said battle of Gettysburg; that this deponent saw said Franklin fall when wounded as aforesaid; that this deponent was also wounded in said engagement and was taken to the Hospital of the 2nd Corps in the field and there saw the said Franklin and his said wound; that said Franklin was in great pain and suffered seriously and was unable to walk or stand or help himself....

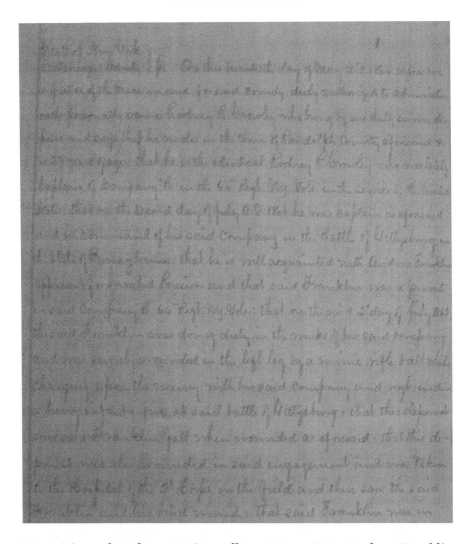

Deposition of Rodney R. Crowell, 20 May 1864, Andres Franklin (Pvt., Co. B, 64th NY Inf., Civil War), pension application no. 81,772, Case Files of Approved Pension Applications, 1861-1934; Civil War and Later Pension Files; National Archives, Washington, D.C.

What They Are

Military records were created by the US government for all branches of the military: army, navy, marines, coast guard, and air force. These consist primarily of service records, and pension records; both should be looked at for any male ancestor who may have been in the military. The National Archives is the repository for millions of documents pertaining to military records, which include logs, registers, service records, court-martial reports, correspondence, case files, and unindexed bounty land warrants, that are not online. Here I am primarily talking about pension records, which worth obtaining for any veteran who obtained benefits.

In looking for real examples, written by our ancestors, telling what life was like for them, military pension records are wonderful for giving us a glimpse into the past. When a soldier was disabled by injuries suffered during his service or afterwards, in many cases he, his parents, widow, and/or children could apply for a pension. Pension records in the United States begin with soldiers of the Revolutionary War, as a reward for the service given. Before 1818 the pensions were given for injuries suffered during service; after 1818 the injury or disability did not have to be as a result of the service.

Over the years Congress passed several different laws relating to pension records and how soldiers or their dependents could qualify. If your male ancestor was between the ages of 16 and 60 during any major American conflict, be sure to look for a pension record!

Valuable Information

Pension records are especially rich in genealogical information; often the soldier had to provide proof of his service, through military records or depositions from friends who served with him. If his widow was applying for a pension for herself or her children, she had to provide proof of their marriage and the dates of birth for the children. This may have taken the form of depositions from ministers or town clerks, or from the midwife who delivered the children. There may be depositions from family members who can say, "I was there at the wedding." Many times (even though they were instructed not to send originals) the soldiers and their families sent in Bible records and photographs in order to try to prove their case.

While the majority of Revolutionary War pension records have been digitized and are online at Fold3 (http://www.fold3.com); the pension records for later conflicts are not. The National Archives is in the process of digitizing the War of 1812 pension records, which are also online at Fold3. It may be several months before this project is complete, so if you suspect an ancestor may have fought in the War of 1812, it's worth investigating.

Levi Lane of Watertown, Connecticut, fought in the War of 1812, and died in 1872. His widow Susan died October 1886. In his pension file is a fairly complete record of his military service, a physical description ("dark brown hair, blue eyes, about five feet and eight inches in height"), and evidence that he received a Land Warrant.

Among the items in this file is a note dated 1813, stating that he is unwell and should be excused from military service:

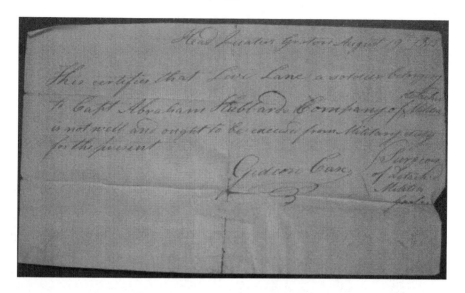

Levi Lane (Pvt., Capt. Abraham Hubbard's Co., Conn. Militia, War of 1812), pension application no. 26680, Case Files of Approved Pension Applications, 1871-1900; War of 1812 Pension and Bounty Land Warrant Application Files; National Archives, Washington, D.C.

There is also a deposition by the Judge of Probate for Watertown, Connecticut:

This certifies that I have now in my possession the family Bible of Levi Lane and Susan Lane – which Bible was printed in Hartford by Hudson & Goodwin in the year 1812 as appears on the title page – in which appears the following Record, "March 6th A.D. 1817 Levi Lane Married to Sukey Hotchkiss."

Deposition of Allyn M. Hungerford, 10 May 1878, Levi Lane (Pvt., Capt. Abraham Hubbard's Co., Conn. Militia, War of 1812), pension application no. 26680, Case Files of Approved Pension Applications, 1871-1900; War of 1812 Pension and Bounty Land Warrant Application Files; National Archives, Washington, D.C.

In the Civil War pension file for John Chaffin, who was a chaplain for the 59th Ohio Volunteer Infantry, there is a postcard from his widow, who was living in Tacoma, Washington in 1921:

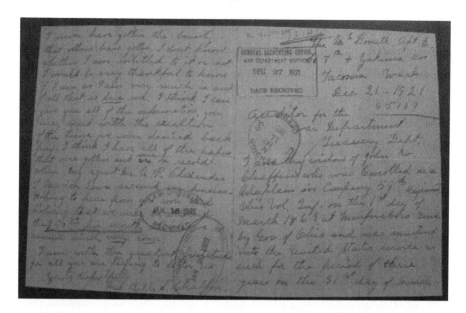

Belle Chaffin postcard, 21 December 1921, John W. Chaffin (Chaplain, Co. F, 59th OH V.I.), pension application no. 542,669, Case Files of Approved Pension Applications, 1861-1934; Civil War and Later Pension Files; National Archives, Washington, D.C.

The Civil War pension file of Henry R. Jones, of Hillsdale, Michigan, is fascinating. He applied for and received a pension, and after he died, two women came forward, both claiming to be his widow. The index card to this huge, 200+ page file is online at Ancestry:

"Civil War Pension Index: General Index to Pension Files, 1861-1934," digital image; *Ancestry* (http://www.ancestry.com: accessed 9 August 2013); Henry R. Jones (Co. B, 2nd MI Cav.) index card; imaged from *General Index to Pension Files, 1861-1934*, T288 (Washington, D.C.: National Archives).

In this file, there are depositions from both women. Orinda McMullin Jones, the widow who was living with Henry when he died, stated that she was pretty sure both of her previous husbands were deceased, but couldn't prove it. She also listed all the places she had lived during her life:

What was your maiden name?
Claimant: Orinda Maria McMullin. I was born in Jannoque, Province of Ontario, Can. in 1835, I lived there until 8 years of age. Then for two years I lived with my sister Sabra wife of Miles Hutchinson, at Alexander Bay, Jefferson Co. NY then I lived with mother again, about a year. Her Christian name was Dorothy, and she had remarried to William Chapel. Then I lived with a sister, Jane wife of Abel Runyons at Oswego, NY a little less than a year.

Deposition of Orinda Jones, 15 January 1903, Henry R. Jones (Co. B, 2nd MI Cav.), pension application no. 760,630, Case Files of Approved Pension Applications, 1861-1934; Civil War and Later Pension Files; National Archives, Washington, D.C.

As it turned out, neither Orinda nor Lizzie got the pension – Orinda because she could not prove that her previous two husbands were deceased, and Lizzie because her "marriage" to Henry took place when she was much younger than 16 and therefore was not valid.

Where to Find Military Pension Records

Military Pension Records are federal records, and as such they will be found in the National Archives in Washington, D.C. The index cards to these pension records are online at Fold3 and Ancestry; you will need the pension numbers in order to request the pension records. Be sure to make a note of ALL of the pension numbers, and know that "S" stands for soldier and "W" for widow.

While you can order these records online from the National Archives, they are expensive, and there is no guarantee you will receive the whole file. My suggestion is to hire a researcher who can take digital photographs of these fragile documents. (See Getting Help).

These pension records are full of information, and won't be totally online for some time yet. Take the time to go after them!

Divorce Records

In the papers I received from my grandfather's estate, he had written this about his grandfather, James Lawrence Reed:

> *James Reed, who was my grandfather, married once more, this time to his first wife's sister, Dora Curtis Phillips. Both parties were old people at the time, in their 70's, and although they had expected to be supremely happy n a really romantic marriage, it did not turn out that way. He went out to Seattle where she had a house, and set up his shoe shop, for he was a cobbler all his life. They were too set in their ways, however, and did not agree, so the shoe shop was soon sold out and J.L. returned to Michigan.*

Once I figured out a time frame for the divorce (thanks to newspaper articles from *The Olympia Daily Recorder* in 1915, published online), I went to the Washington State Archives in Olympia and asked to see the record. The archivist brought me a file that was three inches thick, and full of amazing paperwork, including affidavits from friends and relatives of the defendant, James L. Reed, recorded by a notary public in Benzonia, Michigan:

Dora A. Reed
    Plaintiff.)
)   NO 6098
 -vs-   )
)   Order.
James L.Reed.   )
    Defendant.)

Before me Florin Benedict a Notary Public in and for the

County of Benzie and State of Michigan, personally appeared

James L.Reed, Percy A.Reed, and Carl M.Tinkham at 2 ocolck PM

on the 15th day of May 1916. and answered the interrogatories

numerically as propounded in the order of the superior court

of the State of Washington in and for the County of Thurston.

James L.Reed the defendant first being du-ly sworn answering

says,

Answer to Question 1   Yes.

Answer to Question 2 My Age is 76, and I reside in

Beulah, Benzie County Mich.

Answer to Question 3 Yes. in 1863.I married Ellen Curtis,

Answer to Question 4. I became aquainted with the Plaintiff

in 1861 at Berrien County Mich.

Answer to Question 5 I had about $1000 in money at thetime

of our marriage.about $800 of which was used in the purchase

ofthe house and lot and in repairs for the same the bal-ance

Dora A. Reed vs. James L. Reed, case 6098, 1916; Divorce case files, affidavit of James L. Reed taken in Beulah, Benzie County, Michigan on 15 May 1916; Washington State Archives, Olympia, WA.

Even though I knew a lot about my great-grandfather's life, this file was full of first-hand information, including the date and place of James Reed's first marriage to my great-grandmother Mary Ellen Curtis.

What They Are

Divorce records are the court papers that are the legal record of the dissolution of a marriage. Sometimes we have a false image of the past as a divorce-free zone, where all couples, happy or not, stayed together for life. Unfortunately (or maybe fortunately for us!) that was not the case.

Valuable Information

Divorce records usually contain:

the initial lawsuit by the plaintiff, either husband or wife, stating the charges

the date and place of the marriage

the names and ages/birthdates of any children of the marriage

arrangements for child support or alimony

proof that the charges were served against the defendant

affidavits from one or both of the parties answering the charges

depositions by witnesses testifying on behalf of either party

the decree of divorce, signed by the judge

any requests for changes in child support or custody

When John B. Painter applied for a pension for his service as a Civil War soldier, he needed to provide a record of his 1874 marriage to his second wife, Margaret Sadler. However, a record of that marriage couldn't be found, so they needed to be married again in 1890. In order to do that, he needed a record of his divorce from his first wife, Sarah Wood.

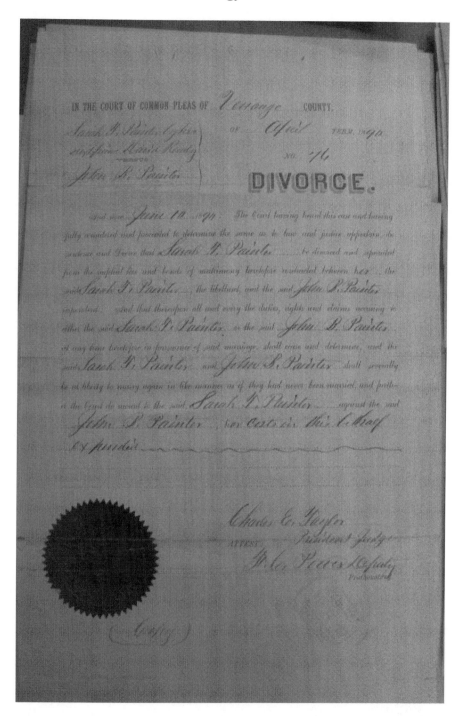

Venango County, Pennsylvania, Court of Common Pleas, Decree of Divorce for Sarah T. Painter v. John B. Painter, no. 76 (1890), John B. Painter (Co. C, 6th PA H.A.), pension application no. 267,186), Case Files of Approved Pension Applications, 1861-1934; Civil War and Later Pension Files; National Archives, Washington, D.C.

Where to Find Divorce Records

Divorce records are court documents, and will be filed first of all in the county where the divorce took place. They will usually be indexed in the civil case files. Older case files may have been transferred to the state archives.

County courthouses

At the Lewis County clerk's office in Chehalis, Washington, the divorce records are available by requesting them by name and date. Once the clerk finds the record, the resulting image is brought up on the research computer.

In 1925, fire chief E.C. Kuehner filed for divorce, stating that his wife Margaret were married in July 1922, and had one child, two-year old Margaret Louise Kuehner.

They had been residents of Lewis County, Washington for more than three years. He asked for, and received custody of his daughter, and the file contained records of changes in the custody arrangements after Margaret entered nurses training at the Tacoma General Hospital. This file is not on microfilm at the Family History Library.

Lewis County, Washington, Court Clerk, 20:158, E.C. Kuehner v. Margaret Kuehner (1925); digital image; Lewis County Law & Justice Center, Chehalis, Washington.

In Susquehanna County, Pennsylvania in 1858, John Austin entered a petition for divorce from his wife, saying that she had left him almost two years earlier. This file (not on microfilm) includes the initial complaint, proof of service to Mary Austin, depositions from John's grown children from a prior marriage, and the decree of divorce.

Susquehanna county, Pennsylvania, Prothonotary's Office, Court of Common Pleas Docket 22:574 John Austin v. Mary Austin (1859), Montrose, Pennsylvania.

In October of 1892 the saga of Jack Dana and Catherine Helmer entertained the readers of the Tacoma Daily News. They were married after a whirlwind courtship, but it turned out there was a little matter of Jack's previous marriage which may or may not have been legally dissolved. Catherine promptly filed for divorce, and the record is on microfilm at the Pierce County clerk's office.

Family History Library

The Family History Library in Salt Lake City, Utah, has many court records on microfilm. For example, the divorce records from 1852 to 1921 for Clackamas County, Oregon are on 60 rolls of microfilm, indexed and arranged by surname:

Title
Divorces, 1852–1921; index, 1852–1920, Clackamas County, Oregon

Authors
Oregon. Circuit Court (Clackamas County) (Main Author)

Notes
Microfilm of original records at the Oregon State Archives in Salem, Oregon.
Arranged in alphabetical order by name of plaintiff.
Includes index. Index lists name, case number, year, and type of case.
Some case numbers are missing and were not microfilmed.

Subjects
Oregon, Clackamas - Divorce records

Format
Manuscript (On Film)

Language
English

Publication
Salt Lake City, Utah : Filmed by the Genealogical Society of Utah, 1999

Physical
60 microfilm reels ; 35 mm.

Film Notes
Note - Location [Film]
Index to divorces, case files #1-9999, 1852-1910 - FHL US/CAN Film [2169230 Item 1]
Index to divorces, case files #10000-17600, 1910-1920 - FHL US/CAN Film [2169739 Item 2]
Abercrombie, Flora vs. Abercrombie, William to Becker, William vs. Becker, Anna - FHL US/CAN Film [2169230 Item 2]
Beebe, Mabel vs. Beebe, Ellsworth to Brown, Mary A. vs. Brown, Charles J. - FHL US/CAN Film [2169231]
Brown, Mary J. vs. Brown, Thomas J. to Chase, Clara A. vs. Chase, Edward S. - FHL US/CAN Film [2169297]

Genealogy Offline:

On 9 March 1909, Minnie Brownell came before the Clackamas County, Oregon circuit court requesting a divorce, stating that her husband Francis M. Brownell was not supporting her and their four children, enforcing her to put the children in the Children's Home, paying $25 a month for their care. In this complaint she states the date and place of their marriage (30 December 1894 in Scott County, Minnesota), and the names and ages of their four minor children.

```
 1   of March,A.D.1908, while the said plaintiff was out washing, scrubbing
 2   and doing general housework, said defendant neglected to take any in-
 3   trest in the children or try to keep them from running on the street
 4   and out of mischief and,through his lack of attention, the children
 5   became so neglected that the plaintiff herein was compelled to place
 6   them in the Children's Home, so that they would receive proper care
 7   and attention and the said plaintiff has been compelled to contribute
 8   the sum of Twenty Five($25.00) Dollars, per month for their support.
 9                              VI
10       That to enable the plaintiff herein to provide for her children, she
11   has been compelled to seek employment as domestic and housekeeper as said
12   defendant, disregarding the solemnity of his marriage vow, willfully and
13   without cause has deserted and abandoned the plaintiff and ever since and
14   still continues so to do willfully and without cause desert and abandon
15   said plaintiff and to live separate and apart from her without any suf-
16   ficient cause or reason and against her will and consent.
17       WHEREFORE, the plaintiff asks this Court for a decree dissolving the
18   marriage contract heretofore existing between said plaintiff and defendant
19   and the care and custody of her four minor children and her costs and dis-
20   bursements herein incurred and such other and further relief as in equity
21   may seem meet and unto justice appertained.
22
23                              _____
                                Attorney for Plaintiff
24   Page 2 Complaint.
```

Clackamas County Circuit Court, case no. 9268, Minnie B. Brownell vs. Francis M. Brownell (1909), FHL microfilm 2169297.

Sometimes divorce records raise more questions than they answer. Also in this file is a notice from the judge, dated 21 February 1914, that the case was dismissed because neither of the attorneys showed up for the hearing!

In any court case, the attorneys for the plaintiff (person filing the petition for divorce) were charged with doing everything they could to let the defendant know about the petition, so they could present their side of the story. Often this summons was delivered in person, and sometimes a notice was published in the local newspaper.

Clackamas County, Oregon, circuit court case no.7137, Hettie Clarke vs. George Clark (1901), FHL microfilm 2169298.

Generally, in order to find a divorce record you will need to know where the couple was living, in order to access the court records from that place and time.

Divorce records are another important record for a complete family history.

Adoption & Guardianship Records

When I found my great great grandfather Stacy Clay Thompson on the 1900 census of Manistee, Michigan, I was puzzled to find a family member that had not appeared in any other records. Florence M. Thompson, age 6, was listed as an adopted daughter. By the 1910 census, she had disappeared. Who was she, and what happened to her?

An online resource, US GenWeb, provided a clue. On the Manistee county website was a probate index with a listing for Florence Marie Thompson that gave a file number.

```
Thomas, George 1042-541
Thomas, Wm. 456-233
Thompson, Anthony 229-117
Thompson, Catharine McAughey 1025-523
Thompson, Florence Marie 1205-613
Thompson, Isaac 228-116
Thompson, Lucy 1166-593
Thompson, Nina 476-244
Thompson, Ole 697-357
Thorp, Charles J. 243-124
Thorp, Margaret E. 58-30
```

Name Index to Manistee Probate Court Calendar "B", *Manistee County GenWeb* (http://www.rootsweb.ancestry.com/~mimanist/ManProbateCalB.html: accessed 3 August 2013), transcribed from FHL microfilm 945560.

Not content to wait for the microfilm, I wrote to the Manistee County Courthouse, and received copies of the paperwork. It told a fascinating story.

Stacy Clay Thompson's son-in-law Herbert Randall had a sister, Eliza (Randall) Udell, who was recently widowed and could not take care of her youngest daughter, Almira Louise. Stacy and his wife Ida May offered to adopt the little girl, and they did so in 1897, changing her name to Florence Marie Thompson. By the time Ida May Thompson died in 1906, Eliza Udell had remarried and was in better financial circumstances, and wanted her daughter back.

APPLICATION FOR ADOPTION AND CHANGE OF NAME OF A MINOR.   (630)   [printer's imprint]

Know all Men by these Presents, That we, *Garrett L. Johnson*
and *Eliza May Johnson* his wife, of the
of , County of , State of Michigan,
do hereby declare that *Florence Marie Thompson*

a minor child of *Stacey C. Thompson and Ida M. Thompson*
deceased, by adoption,
of the age of *thirteen*
years on the *11th* day of *August*, 19*26*, is adopted
by us, and each of us, as our child, and that we intend to make such child, so adopted, our heir and the
heir of each of us, and desire that such child shall hereafter bear our family name, to-wit: the name of
Florence Marie Johnson
And we, the said *Garrett L. Johnson and Eliza May Johnson*

do each of us declare that this instrument is executed in good faith, and we do hereby request the Judge
of Probate for the County of *Manistee* and State of Michigan, to make and enter
in the journal of said Court an order that said *Garrett L. Johnson*
and *Eliza May Johnson* his wife, do stand in the place
of Parents to said child, and that said child be their heir at law, and that the name of such child be
changed as aforesaid, in accordance with the provisions of the Statute in such case made and provided.
And *I, Stacey C. Thompson*
being *the surviving Father Parent of said Minor*

, do execute this instrument for the purpose of giving my
consent in writing to the adoption and change of name of said child as aforesaid, and that said child may
become the heir-at-law of said parties so adopting her.

And said child being above the age of ten
years, hereby joins in the execution of this
instrument for the purpose of consenting to
her adoption and change of name aforesaid

In Testimony Whereof, We have hereunto set our hands and seals, this *13th*
day of *August* 19*26*

Garrett L. Johnson [L.S.]
Eliza May Johnson [L.S.]
Stacey C. Thompson [L.S.]
Florence Marie Thompson [L.S.]
[L.S.]

Adoption petition for Florence M. Thompson, Manistee County
Probate Court, Manistee, Michigan

What They Are

Adoption records are the court papers recording the adoption of a child. In the United States, adoption became a formal legal act when Massachusetts passed a law covering the process of adoption in 1851. The first law concerning the confidentiality of adoption records was passed in Minnesota in 1917.

Each state has its own statutes that cover adoption. The Revised Code of Washington, Chapter 26.33.40 states that there will be limited disclosure of information. In county courthouses in Washington, adoption cases may be listed in the index of Civil court cases, but the files themselves are not included on the microfilm.

Guardianship records are the records of one or more adults who were appointed to be guardians of children who had lost one (or both) parents, or of adults who were not capable of taking care of themselves.

Valuable Information

The court records of an adoption, if available, may show the child's name and birth date or age, and the names of the birth parents, if known. The adoptive parents would sign an agreement that they would care for the child as their own, and if the child was over a certain age, the child would also sign. In the case of Florence Marie Thompson above, Florence was older than ten so she signed the agreement along with the adults.

Just as children could be adopted, or have guardians appointed, when they are not able to take care of themselves, sometimes older people needed to have guardians to handle their affairs. When it was obvious to his Bear Lake, Michigan neighbors that Henry Chase's mind was slipping, his son-in-law Maurice Reed petitioned and was appointed his guardian by the Manistee County Probate Court. The 75-page file includes signed acknowledgements from both of Henry's daughters, giving the guardianship to Maurice, correspondence between Maurice and the court regarding Henry's property, a yearly accounting of receipts and expenses, and the papers authorizing him to be admitted to the Traverse City State Hospital.

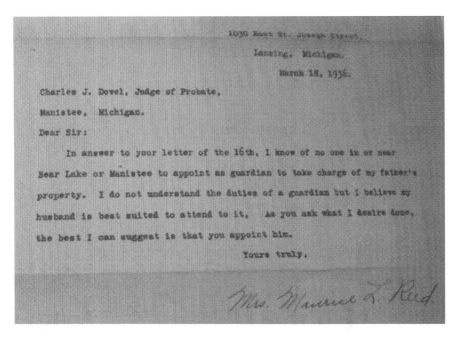

Manistee County Probate Court, case no. 1093-F, Henry H. Chase, mentally incompetent (1936), Manistee, Michigan.

Where to Find Adoption & Guardianship Records

Court records were often microfilmed and if so, are listed in the Family History Library online catalog. Be aware, however, that just because they're on microfilm and in the catalog is no guarantee you'll be able to view them. The owning agency can, and does, put restrictions on the records they allow to be filmed. Some microfilms will never be digitized and put online because of those restrictions. Some films, such as the ones I've listed here, are not available for viewing.

Adoption records (San Miguel County, New Mexico), 1872-1889, 1900-1924, Film 1734598, item 6

Certificate of adoption, V1, 1900-1924 (San Miguel County, New Mexico), Film 1542782, item 4

Both of these microfilms are in the Granite Vault, and are not available for use.

However, some adoptions, especially if they took place before 1900, are available in court records.

In Oxford County, Maine, George Waterhouse went to court because he wanted to formally adopt Minnie Bryant, his wife's daughter from a previous marriage:

Oxford County, Maine, Probate Court, Guardianship and Adoption Records 1812-1895, Minnie L. Bryant (1887), FHL microfilm 1183336.

In Eau Claire County, Wisconsin in 1879, Thomas and Mary Randall came to the court "desirous to adopt" Laura Eva Hathaway. Laura's birth parents were named, and the adoptive parents stated that her mother's whereabouts were unknown, and her father did not live in Wisconsin; Laura's uncle gave permission for the adoption.

412

Eau Claire County Court. For Probate.

In the matter of the adoption of
Laura Eva Hathaway
by Thomas E. Randall
and Mary A. Randall his Wife.

Upon reading and filing the petition of Thomas
E. Randall and Mary A. Randall his Wife, from which
it appears that the said Laura Eva Hathaway is
a child of Benjamin F. Hathaway and Lizzie
Hathaway his Wife, both now residents of the State of
Wisconsin; that said Laura Eva Hathaway is an
infant under the age of fourteen years and was
nine (9) years of age on the 30th day of January
A.D. 1879; that said Thomas E. Randall and
Mary A. Randall his Wife, are desirous to adopt
said infant as their child; and the whereabouts
of the mother of said child is unknown, and
that the father of said child is not a resident
of this State. and Corydon L. Beardsley grand
uncle of and next of kin to said child within
this State, having given his consent in writing to
such adoption, and this Court being satisfied
of the identity and relations of the persons, and that
said petitioners are of sufficient ability to bring
up and furnish suitable nurture and education
for said child, having reference to the degree and
condition of its parents, and that it is proper that
such adoption shall take effect;
It is Ordered, that from and after hereof said
Laura Eva Hathaway shall be deemed to all
legal intents and purposes the child of the petitioners
Thomas E. Randall and Mary A. Randall his
Wife, and that the name of said child be changed to
Laura Eva Randall according to the prayer of
said petition.
Dated this 10th day of March 1879.
By the Court.
A. C. Ellis

Eau Claire County, Wisconsin, Probate Record Book A:412, Laura Hathaway (1879), FHL microfilm 1314840.

Even though today we are used to having adoption records being sealed, that wasn't always the case. If you suspect an adoption or guardianship took place in your family history, it's worth exploring!

Newspapers

A few years ago I was visiting the Manistee County Historical Museum in Manistee, Michigan, a treasure trove of artifacts, photographs and historic information about life in Northern Michigan over 100 years ago. I happened to mention to the director that I'd never found an obituary for my great-grandfather Henry Chase, who had lived in Bear Lake for decades. He asked me the name and date, and disappeared downstairs into the basement. Before too long, he came upstairs with the original copy of the *Manistee County Pioneer Press* for Friday, September 13, 1940, and right there on the front page was the obituary I needed.

"Henry H. Chase, Oldtime Bear Laker, Died Wednesday," *Manistee County Pioneer Press*, 13 September 1940, p. 1, col. 4.

I would not have found this obituary by looking online. Manistee has decades of newspaper publishing history, often publishing 4 different papers during the same time period; but at this point the only issues online are at Google News, and cover the period 1871-1890. And they are not indexed!

What They Are

Newspapers have been published in this country since the 1690's, when *Publick Occurances* was published in Boston. and many of the newspapers of the past have been digitized and put online. They range from big-city dailies to once-a-week rural papers consisting of four pages, and in their day were the primary method of receiving local and national news.

Be sure to look at newspapers not just for obituaries or marriage announcements, but also for other happenings in the community. Announcements of family reunions, work promotions, retirement, and wedding anniversaries can all contribute to your knowledge. Reading the newspaper from the time and place your ancestor lived can give you a real feel for what their lives were like.

Valuable Information

Newspapers should never be overlooked as a source of good information about your ancestors. Often they would publish photographs, especially if a person was a prominent, well-known and/or well-loved member of the community. This photo of Andrew Felt, who was born in Sweden and died in 1929 at the age of 93 was obtained for me by a researcher at the Minnesota Historical Society:

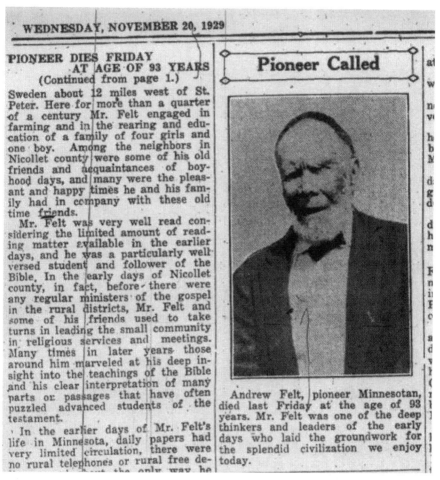

PIONEER DIES FRIDAY AT AGE OF 93 YEARS

(Continued from page 1.)

Sweden about 12 miles west of St. Peter. Here for more than a quarter of a century Mr. Felt engaged in farming and in the rearing and education of a family of four girls and one boy. Among the neighbors in Nicollet county were some of his old friends and acquaintances of boyhood days, and many were the pleasant and happy times he and his family had in company with these old time friends.

Mr. Felt was very well read considering the limited amount of reading matter available in the earlier days, and he was a particularly well-versed student and follower of the Bible. In the early days of Nicollet county, in fact, before there were any regular ministers of the gospel in the rural districts, Mr. Felt and some of his friends used to take turns in leading the small community in religious services and meetings. Many times in later years those around him marveled at his deep insight into the teachings of the Bible and his clear interpretation of many parts or passages that have often puzzled advanced students of the testament.

In the earlier days of Mr. Felt's life in Minnesota, daily papers had very limited circulation, there were no rural telephones or rural free de-

Pioneer Called

Andrew Felt, pioneer Minnesotan, died last Friday at the age of 93 years. Mr. Felt was one of the deep thinkers and leaders of the early days who laid the groundwork for the splendid civilization we enjoy today.

"Pioneer Dies Friday at the Age of 93 Years," *St. Peter Herald,* 20 November 1929.

Remember that a newspaper account is only as accurate as the information provided to it by the informant. Sometimes what is not said in a newspaper is just as important as what is mentioned. When Claudia Thompson Randall died in Detroit in October 1931, her obituary in the Manistee News-Advocate just mentions her son, but not her daughter or 3-month old granddaughter living in Detroit, possibly providing evidence to verify a family story about an estrangement.

FORMER RESIDENT DIES AT DETROIT

Mrs. Claudia Randall, Daughter of S. C. Thompson, Passes

Mrs. Claudia G. Randall, wife of Herbert K. Randall, and a daughter of S. C. Thompson, local realtor, died at her home in Detroit yesterday afternoon following an illness of nearly one year.

The body will be brought here for burial in the family lot in Oak Grove cemetery and brief services will be held at the home of her father at 365 First street, Friday afternoon at 2 o'clock.

Mrs. Randall was born in Manistee in 1875 and resided here until 10 years ago when the family moved to Detroit. Her mother, Ida M. Thompson, preceded her in death in 1906. She is survived by her husband, a son Ray, a brother Walter S. Thompson of Detroit, a sister, Bessie B. Porter of Oakland, Calif., and her father in this city.

"Former Resident Dies at Detroit," *Manistee News-Advocate*, 28 October 1931.

Even if you've found your person in a newspaper article online, it's often worth the time to explore other area newspapers that are available only on microfilm.

In 1911 Nellie Curtis of Tacoma was planning to be married, only to have her intended groom break it off by pretending to be robbed. There is one article online about the event, "Imposter Exposed Upon Wedding Eve," from the *Seattle Daily Times* of 6 January 1911.

A look at the Tacoma Daily Ledger, on microfilm at the Tacoma Public Library, tells a slightly different tale. First of all, the newspaper jumped the gun by publishing an account of the "pretty wedding":

> A pretty wedding was solemnized last evening at the home of the bride's parents, Mr. and Mrs. Levander Curtis, when Miss Nellie Curtis and Gerald Gage of Balboa, Cal., were united in marriage. The ceremony took place at 8 o'clock in the presence of family relatives and intimate friends and was followed by an informal reception and collation. Late in the evening the bridal couple left on their wedding trip and will make their home in Balboa.

"Society," *Tacoma Daily Ledger*, 5 January 1911, p.7, col. 3.

The following day they published a lurid account of the breakup:

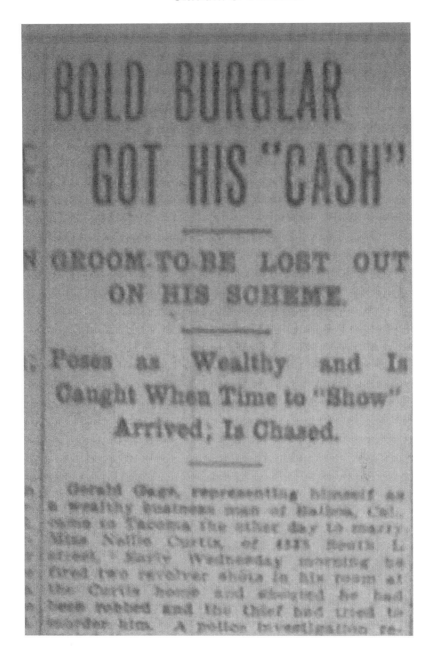

"Bold Burglar Got His "Cash"," *Tacoma Daily Ledger*, 6 January 1911, p.4, col. 3.

Where to Find Local Newspapers

There are a number of ways to discover the titles and repositories for newspapers that were published in your ancestor's neighborhood. Many of these tools are online. For example, you can Google the name of the town or county where your ancestor lived, and add "public library". Often, public libraries will have historic newspapers on microfilm. Look on their website for a Local History collection, or at the very least a contact email or phone number. I have gotten printed copies and digital copies of newspaper articles (free or for a small fee) from libraries just by emailing and asking.

In 1916 in a small town in Pennsylvania, Paul Lapcevik shot and killed his wife Sarah. I looked up the nearest library online, and found an obituary index at the Adams Memorial Library:

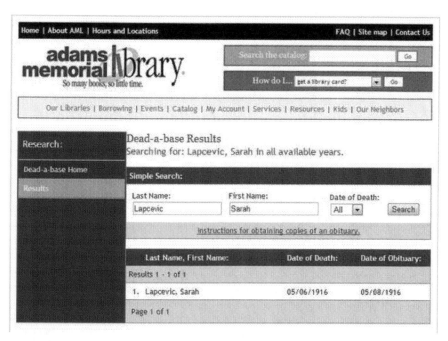

I emailed the library, and they were able to look up the obituary on microfilm, print it out and send it to me, for a charge of $3.

Many libraries, such as the Tacoma Public Library in Washington, or the Medina Library in Ohio have obituary databases where you can look up names. The Wilsonville Library in Clackamas County, Oregon has a downloadable PDF index of obituaries on their website:

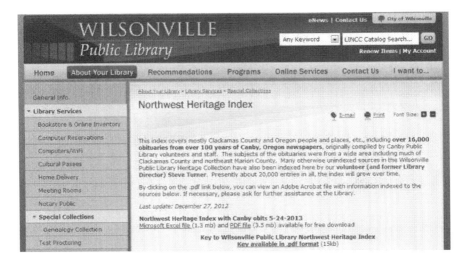

Which actually covers more than just obituaries, but is an index to names and other events.

Be sure to look up anyone else with the last name you're interested in! You may be able to get more pieces of the puzzle by expanding your search beyond just your person of interest.

Another way to find newspaper titles is to use WorldCat (http://www.worldcat.org). This is an online library catalog for contributing libraries, worldwide. In the search screen on their home page, type in the town and state and search "Everything". Here, I am searching for everything on the town of Prosser, Washington:

WorldCat (http://www.worldcat.org: accessed 4 Aug 2013)

On the next screen (with over 1500 results) you can check "Newspaper" to narrow your search. This brings my search results down to 15 titles:

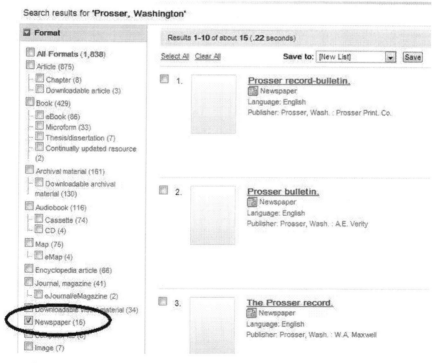

Search results for "Prosser, Washington," *WorldCat* (http://www.worldcat.org: accessed 4 Aug 2013)

From here, you can click on a newspaper title and see which libraries (such as the Washington State Library and the University of Washington) own it. Often libraries will loan out their newspapers on microfilm to your library.

Even if a library (such as the Library of Michigan) will not loan out newspapers, you can still look up newspaper titles in their catalog to see what's covered in your town of interest.

The Library of Michigan has 23 newspaper titles that pertain to Manistee County; each entry describes the library's holdings of that particular title.

When you find the newspaper that covers your time period, if you have an exact date for an event (such as a marriage or obituary), then you can request it through interlibrary loan. If the library will not loan their microfilm, often they will mail you a copy of the article. Interlibrary loan is a genealogist's dream!

Another tool for finding what newspapers have been published in your state is the Library of Congress Chronicling America website, which has a U.S. Newspaper Directory from 1690 to the present.

http://chroniclingamerica.loc.gov/search/titles/

In this directory, if I look up newspapers that were published in Greenhills, Hamilton County, Ohio (a suburb of Cincinnati), I get these results:

US Newspaper Directory Search Results

Results 1 - 4 of 4   Jump to page: [1   ] [GO]

Your title search returned 4 results

Sort by: [Relevance ▼]   Results per page: [20 ▼]

1. Greenhills tribune. (Greenhills, Ohio) 194?-1959
2. North Hills tribune. (Greenhills, Ohio) 1959-197?
3. Greenhills journal. (Greenhills, Ohio) 1950-1962
4. Greenhills-Forest Park journal. (Greenhills [Ohio]) 1962-197?

State archives and state libraries often have complete collections of that state's historic newspapers on microfilm; where they are located differs from state to state. Here in Washington they are housed at the Washington State Library; in Oregon the collection is at the University of Oregon in Eugene. Ohio's historic newspapers (with a valuable online finding aid) are at the Ohio Historical Society. When you're looking for newspapers in a particular state, check the state archives and major universities.

It is encouraging that newspapers are coming online more and more rapidly these days, but keep in mind that there are many more that are not online yet. Newspapers may be kept in the local historical society, the local library, or the state library. They may be on microfilm, or in the original format.

Naturalization Records

When I wanted to know more about my immigrant great-grandfather Johann Stoelt, and particularly when he arrived in Michigan, I looked online at the Archives of Michigan index to naturalization records. A researcher printed the Petition for Naturalization and sent it – and I was surprised that Johann Stoelt entered the United States through Ontario, Canada, not through New York as I'd always supposed. This document also gives his date and place of birth, his wife's name, and the names and birthdates of his children.

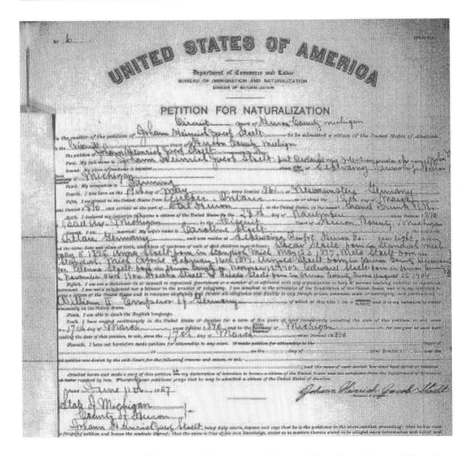

Huron County, Michigan, Johann Stoelt Petition for Naturalization (1907); Michigan State Archives, Lansing.

What They Are

Naturalization records and the laws that create them have changed over the years. When immigrants came to this country and settled, if they wanted to become American citizens they would have to go through a process to accomplish that. Before 1906, any local court (municipal, county, or state) could grant citizenship. After 1906, the naturalization process was handled in the federal courts.

Valuable Information

Naturalization records often have quite a bit of information, such as the person's date and place of birth, the date they arrived in the United States, the name of the ship, and names and birthdates of a spouse and any children.

Where to Find Naturalization Records

Begin your search for naturalization records with the state archives, for records prior to 1906. As mentioned before, the Archives of Michigan has records on microfilm for certain counties, and the indexes to these are available (in PDF format) on their website:

http://seekingmichigan.org/about/indexes

In some states, such as Minnesota, naturalization records are held by the state historical society. When I requested the naturalization record for Andrew Felt, I received a photocopy of the page, which included an affidavit from a friend:

State of Minnesota, | THE DISTRICT COURT, *Ninth* Judicial District. | ss.

County of Nicollet. | Regular Special Term, 1881

Andrew Felt _____ being duly sworn, says, that for the continued term of five years last past, he has resided within the United States, without being at any time, during the said five years, out of the territory of the United States, and that for one year last past, he has resided within the State of Minnesota; and that, at the time he so arrived in the United States, he had attained his eighteenth year.

Sworn in open Court, this 16 day of *July*, 1881, before me. | *Andrew Felt*

Benj Rogers, clerk.

I, *Andrew Felt* _____ do solemnly swear, that I will support the Constitution of the United States, and that I do absolutely and entirely renounce and abjure all allegiance and fidelity to any foreign Prince, Potentate, State or Sovereignty whatever, and particularly to *King of Sweden and Norway* _____ of whom I have heretofore been a subject.

Sworn and subscribed to before me, this 16th day of *July*, 1881 | *Andrew Felt*

Benj Rogers Clerk

State of Minnesota, | ss.

County of Nicollet. | *J B Sackett and L A Graah*

of the County of *Nicollet* _____ and State of *Minnesota* _____, being duly sworn, doth depose and say that he is a citizen of the United States; that he is well acquainted with the above named *Andrew Felt* _____; and that the said *Andrew Felt* _____ has resided within the limits and under the jurisdiction of the United States, for five years last past, and for one year last past, within the State of Minnesota; and that during the same period he has behaved himself as a man of good moral character, attached to the principles of the Constitution of the United States, and well disposed to the good order and happiness of the same. And he further saith, that, at the time the said *Andrew Felt* _____ arrived in the United States, he had attained his eighteenth year.

Sworn and subscribed to before me, this 16th day of *July*, A. D. 1881 | *J B Sackett*

Benj Rogers Clerk | *L A Graah*

UNITED STATES OF AMERICA.

State of Minnesota, County of Nicollet. | DISTRICT COURT, 9TH JUDICIAL DISTRICT.

And now to wit: At a Regular Special term of said Court, now being held at Saint Peter, in and for the County of Nicollet, and State of Minnesota, upon the foregoing oath and affidavits; and upon the further proof that the said *Andrew Felt* _____ did, before the Clerk of the *District* Court of the County of *Washington*, State of *Minnesota* make the requisite declaration of his intention to become a citizen of the United States, and to renounce all other allegiance, as required by the laws of the United States.

It is Ordered by the Court, that the said *Andrew Felt* _____ be, and he is hereby admitted to be a Citizen of the United States.

By the Court: *Benj Rogers*

Clerk of Said Court.

Dated this 16th day of *July* A.D. 18 81

115

Nicollet county, Minnesota, Naturalization Record, SAM 170, r.3, B:27, Andrew Felt (1881); Minnesota Historical Society, St. Paul.

After 1906 prospective citizens may have chosen to be naturalized in a federal court of law; those records are held by the branches of the National Archives. You can see what branches hold records for your state of interest here:

http://www.archives.gov/locations/

The National Archives branch in Seattle, Washington holds records for Alaska, Idaho, Oregon, Washington and Hawaii. They have the original naturalization papers for citizens who applied in Federal court.

In 1931 Rhoda Catherine MacKenzie filed her Declaration of Intention, stating her residence in Seattle, her date and place of birth, her race (Scotch) and nationality (British), and that she entered the United States by way of Victoria, British Columbia in 1927. This application was accompanied by a photograph.

TRIPLICATE

No. 34166

UNITED STATES OF AMERICA

20-6749

DECLARATION OF INTENTION

(Invalid for all purposes seven years after the date hereof)

In the .... U. S. DISTRICT .... Court

of N.Dist.of Wash. at Seattle,Wash.

I, Rhoda Catherine MacKenzie

now residing at 4617 Fontanelle Seattle King Washington

occupation Teacher , aged 48 years, do declare on oath that my personal description is:

Sex female color white , complexion medium , color of eyes blue

color of hair brown , height 5 feet, 5 inches; weight 180 pounds; visible distinctive marks none

race Scotch ; nationality British

I was born in Kilsyth Canada , on July 25 1882

I am not married. The name of my wife or husband is ....

we were married on .... at .... ; she or he was born at .... on .... entered the United States at .... on .... for permanent residence therein, and now resides at .... I have .... children, and the name, date and place of birth, and place of residence of each of said children are as follows: ....

I have heretofore made a declaration of intention: Number .... at Oakland California U.S.District Court 1914

my last foreign residence was Victoria B.C. Canada

I emigrated to the United States of America from Victoria B.C.

my lawful entry for permanent residence in the United States was at Pt.Angeles Washington

under the name of Rhoda Catherine MacKenzie , on August 14 1927

on the vessel S.S.Olympic

I will, before being admitted to citizenship, renounce forever all allegiance and fidelity to any foreign prince, potentate, state, or sovereignty, and particularly, by name, to the prince, potentate, state, or sovereignty of which I may be at the time of admission a citizen or subject; I am not an anarchist; I am not a polygamist nor a believer in the practice of polygamy; and it is my intention in good faith to become a citizen of the United States of America and to reside permanently therein; and I certify that the photograph affixed to the duplicate and triplicate hereof is a likeness of me: So HELP ME GOD.

Rhoda Catherine MacKenzie

Subscribed and sworn to before me in the office of the Clerk of said Court, at Seattle,Washington this 12th day of January anno Domini 1931. Certification No. 20-6749 from the Commissioner of Naturalization showing the lawful entry of the declarant for permanent residence on the date stated above, has been received by me. The photograph affixed to the duplicate and triplicate hereof is a likeness of the declarant.

[SEAL]

Rhoda Catherine MacKenzie

.... Clerk of the .... Court.

By .... , Deputy Clerk.

Form 2202-L-A.

U. S. DEPARTMENT OF LABOR
NATURALIZATION SERVICE

Rhoda MacKenzie Declaration of Intention (1931), naturalization file no. 34166, Western District of Washington; Records of the District Courts of the United States, Record Group 21; National Archives, Pacific Region, Seattle.

It's important to note here that although this image is online at Ancestry, it does not include the photograph. Even if you've found an image of a document online, if you suspect something is missing, it still pays to go after the original.

And although Ancestry may have the Petitions for Naturalization online, they may not tell the whole story. In the file for John Murison Jamieson (born 1906 in Saskatchewan, Canada), who filed a Declaration of Intent on 4 January 1930, is a letter from the U.S. Department of Justice, Emigration and Naturalization Service, dated 18 October 1954, stating that "the person named below has lost United States citizenship since the date of naturalization."

In a similar fashion, the papers for Severino Schierano, also known as Sam Sano, included a notice from the court "that the petitioner is not a person of good moral character." His initial petition for citizenship in 1933 was turned down for this reason, but in 1941 he applied again. Both of these applications are online at Ancestry, but there is no indication (such as a citizenship certificate) that his application was approved.

Although more and more naturalization records are coming online, be aware that many times they consist of just the final papers. If you want the full file, with the Declaration of Intention, Certificate of Entry, and Certificate of Citizenship, along with any other documents, it's worth it to go after the whole file.

Additional Resources

There are many resources online that can help you find those records you're searching for. Here are a few:

Council of State Archivists,
Directory of State and Territorial Archives and Records Programs
http://www.statearchivists.org/states.htm

United States Genealogy & Historical Society Directory
http://www.censusfinder.com/genealogy-society-directory.htm

Directory of Public Libraries:
http://www.publiclibraries.com

US GenWeb

http://www.usgenweb.org

For Further Reading:

Val D. Greenwood, *The researcher's guide to American Genealogy, 3rd ed.* Baltimore: Genealogical Publishing Co., 2000.

E. Wade Hone, *Land & Property Research in the United States.* Salt Lake City: Ancestry, 2008.

Patricia Law Hatcher, *Locating Your Roots: Discover Your Ancestors Using Land Records.* Cincinnati: Betterway Books, 2003.

Christine Rose, *Courthouse Research for Family Historians,* (San Jose: CR Publications, 2004)

Genealogy Offline:

Guide to Genealogical Research in the National Archives of the United States (Washington, D.C.: National Archives and Records Administration, 2000)

Using the Family History Library Catalog

Getting familiar with the Family History Library catalog is essential for finding documents that are not yet online. To begin, go to FamilySearch: http://www.familysearch.org.

Click on "Search" at the top right. Then click on "Catalog" at the top.

Their Beta catalog still needs work, so I always go to the previous version, which looks like this:

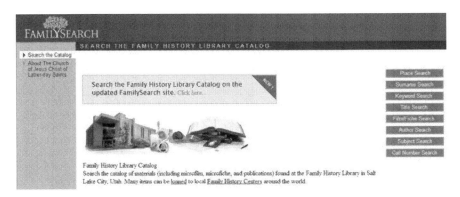

If I want to see what vital records have been microfilmed for Clackamas County, Oregon, I would click on Place Search. I type in the name of the county, and then the name of the state:

Place Search   FAMILY HISTORY LIBRARY CATALOG

Search for matching places.

Place   Clackamas

Part of (optional)   Oregon

[Search]

- In the Place field, type the name of the town, county, or other place that you are looking for.
- To narrow the search, type the name of a larger place in the Part Of field. Exception: Do not type "United States" or "Canada" in the Part of field.
   - To find all towns and counties in the world named Barton, type **Barton** in the Place field, and leave the Part Of field blank.
   - To find all towns in England named Barton, type **Barton** in the Place field and **England** in the Part Of field.
   - To find the town of Barton in the county of Stafford, type **Barton** in the Place field and **Stafford** in the Part Of field.
- For counties, do not type the word "County."

When I click on "Search", I'm presented with a number of possibilities:

Place Search Results

Place (Part of)

clackamas (Oregon)

Place search results

Clackamas

United States, Oregon, Clackamas

United States, Oregon, Clackamas, Clackamas

Clackamas Park

United States, Oregon, Clackamas, Clackamas Park

3 matching places.

Clicking on "Oregon, Clackamas" will give me all the records that the Family History Library has for that county.

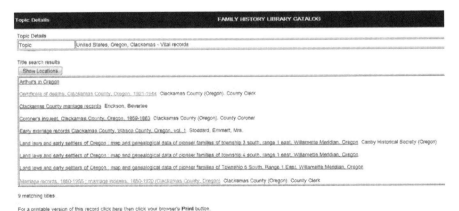

Clicking on "Vital records" will give you this list:

At the bottom it says "9 matching titles", but that does not mean there are only 9 rolls of microfilm for this county!

When you click on the last listing, "Marriage records, 1850-1935", you'll see this screen:

Title Details	FAMILY HISTORY LIBRARY CATALOG
Title	Marriage records, 1850-1935 ; marriage indexes, 1850-1920 (Clackamas County, Oregon)
Authors	Clackamas County (Oregon). County Clerk (Main Author) Oregon. District Court (Clackamas County) (Added Author)
Notes	Microfilm of original records at the Oregon State Archives in Salem, Oregon. Includes index. Index may include name of bride, name of groom, case number, and year of marriage. Some years are missing and were not microfilmed. Some marriage records are arranged in alphabetical order by the surname of the bride.
Subjects	United States, Oregon, Clackamas - Vital records
Format	Manuscript (On Film)
Language	English
Publication	Salt Lake City, Utah : Filmed by the Genealogical Society of Utah, 1999
Physical	on 4 microfilm reels ; 35 mm.

For a printable version of this record click here then click your browser's **Print** button.

This entry says there are 4 rolls of microfilm. In order to find the details and the microfilm numbers, you need to look at the bottom of the screen, where it says "For a printable version of this record click here then click your browser's Print button.:

For a printable version of this record click here then click your browser's **Print** button.

Here you will be able to read the details on this record set, including where the original records are kept, how each book is indexed (or not), and if any years are missing.

Title
Marriage records, 1850-1935 ; marriage indexes, 1850-1920 (Clackamas County, Oregon)

Authors
Clackamas County (Oregon). County Clerk (Main Author)
Oregon. District Court (Clackamas County) (Added Author)

Notes
Microfilm of original records at the Oregon State Archives in Salem, Oregon.
Includes index.
Index may include name of bride, name of groom, case number, and year of marriage.
Some years are missing and were not microfilmed.
Some marriage records are arranged in alphabetical order by the surname of the bride.

Subjects
United States, Oregon, Clackamas - Vital records

Format
Manuscript (On Film)

Language
English

Publication
Salt Lake City, Utah : Filmed by the Genealogical Society of Utah, 1999

Physical
on 4 microfilm reels ; 35 mm.

Film Notes
Note - Location [Film]
Bride - Groom index for marriages, 1850-1920 - FHL US/CAN Film [2171123 Item 1]
Groom - Bride index for marriages, 1850-1920 - FHL US/CAN Film [2171123 Item 2]
Loose marriage records, 1850-1875 - FHL US/CAN Film [2171123 Item 3]
Loose marriage records, 1876-1888 - FHL US/CAN Film [2171124]
Loose marriage records, 1889-1919 (1890-1909, 1913-1914 are missing) - FHL US/CAN Film [2184576]
Loose marriage records, 1920-1935 (1922-1930 are missing) - FHL US/CAN Film [2184577 Item 1]
Marriage records, v. 1-4, 1853-1892 - FHL US/CAN Film [2184577 Items 2 - 5]

Then you will see the Film Notes, which detail the records that are on each microfilm, and the microfilm number.

Physical
on 4 microfilm reels ; 35 mm.

Film Notes
Note - Location [Film]
Bride - Groom index for marriages, 1850-1920 - FHL US/CAN Film [2171123 Item 1]
Groom - Bride index for marriages, 1850-1920 - FHL US/CAN Film [2171123 Item 2]
Loose marriage records, 1850-1875 - FHL US/CAN Film [2171123 Item 3]
Loose marriage records, 1876-1888 - FHL US/CAN Film [2171124]
Loose marriage records, 1889-1919 (1890-1909, 1913-1914 are missing) - FHL US/CAN Film [2184576]
Loose marriage records, 1920-1935 (1922-1930 are missing) - FHL US/CAN Film [2184577 Item 1]
Marriage records, v. 1-4, 1853-1892 - FHL US/CAN Film [2184577 Items 2 - 5]

Looking at this list tells you which microfilm to order. If you don't have an exact date, it's always best to start out with the indexes.

Ordering Family History Library Microfilm Online

The first step in ordering microfilm from the Family History Library is to determine the nearest FamilySearch Center located near you. You can do that by going to
https://familysearch.org/locations/centerlocator
Here you can locate the Family History Center that's most convenient for you, by using the map or typing in an address.

Once you have the film numbers you want to order, and the location of the FHC nearest you, you can go to the page for Online Film Ordering:

https://familysearch.org/films/

Be sure to create an account first, so that you will get a receipt for your payment, and be notified when your film arrives! The cost is $7.50 per roll, and you can pay by debit card or through PayPal.

Getting Help

It's fairly obvious that if I live in Seattle and need a record from the National Archives in Washington DC (or the state library in Lansing, Michigan, or the North Carolina State Archives in Raleigh, NC – you get the idea), I can't drop everything and fly across country at the drop of a hat, no matter how much I might crave that record.

Over the last few years I've developed a network of researchers in many other states (and countries) who will obtain records for me at a reasonable cost. Here's how you can find them:

The Association of Professional Genealogists is "an international organization dedicated to supporting those engaged in the business of genealogy...." and one of the terrific benefits of their website is the APG Directory. Their website is http://www.apgen.org. Here you can search by name, location, and research or geographic specialty. When I'm looking for a researcher in another area, I tend to gravitate toward those who have a professional business website, and display their education, research specialties and qualifications. Chapter websites have lists of their members, contact information and specialties. It doesn't cost anything to email a researcher and ask about their rates and availability to do research for you.

The Board for Certification of Genealogists is an independent organization that certifies genealogists that have shown that they meet rigorous standards. The BCG promotes educational opportunities for all genealogists, and upholds standards. On their website
(http://www.bcgcertification.org) you can search for a genealogist by name, credentials, organization, location, specialties, services and languages.

Accredited Genealogists have to pass thorough written and oral exams given by the International Association for the Accreditation of Professional Genealogists (http://www.icapgen.org). They are accredited by regions, such as Great Plains States, Gulf South, Canadian, American Indian, and overseas areas such as England, Ireland or Sweden. You can also search their directory by name, country, state or city of residence, and area of specialty.

About the Author

Claudia Breland is a professional genealogist with almost 40 years of research experience. She is a member of the Association of Professional Genealogists, the National Genealogical Society, and various state and local genealogical societies. She has written articles for the national website Archives.com, the Association of Professional Genealogists Quarterly, and a column for her community newspaper, the Voice of the Valley. She has done onsite research at state archives in Washington, Oregon, Michigan and North Carolina, and at state libraries and county courthouses across the country.

Claudia has a Master's in Library Science, and has worked in the three largest library systems in Western Washington. She has taught library skills at the community college level, and recently completed coursework for a Paralegal Certificate. For the past three years she has lectured on various topics for her local library system and several genealogical societies.

Claudia's website is http://www.ccbreland.com. You can contact her at ccbreland@comcast.net.

Claudia lives in the Key Peninsula of Washington, near Gig Harbor. This is her first book.

Acknowledgements

I would like to express my heartfelt appreciation to the following mentors and researchers:

Teresa McMillin, CG
Judy G. Russell, CG, CGL
Dr. Thomas W. Jones, CG, CGL, FASG
Elissa Scalise Powell, CG, CGL
Elizabeth Shown Mills, CG, CGL, FASG
Steven W. Morrison, Olympia, WA
Patricia McIntyre, Salt Lake City, UT
Kimberly Powell, Oakdale, PA
Bethany Waterbury, Lansing, MI
Patricia Ann Gillespie, Fredericksburg, VA
Eric Stroschein, Mount Vernon, WA
Members of the Puget Sound Chapter, Association of Professional Genealogists
Ken House, Seattle branch, National Archives & Records Administration
Phil Stairs, Puget Sound Regional Archives, Bellevue, WA

Coming Soon!

To be published in 2014:

Genealogy Offline 2: even more family history records that are not online

1. Letters, Journals and Diaries
2. Manuscripts
3. Photographs
4. School Records
5. Employment Records
6. Funeral Home Records
7. Coroner and Inquest Records
8. Hospital Records
9. Criminal Records
10. City Directories

Made in the USA
Lexington, KY
28 May 2014